Traverse Theatre Company

Gorgeous Avatar

by Jules Horne

cast in order of appearance

Amy	Pauline Knowles
Dan	Patrick Hoffman
Rose	Una McLean
Rafi	John Kazek

Director	Philip Howard
Designer	Mark Leese
Lighting Designer	Kai Fischer
Composer	Jon Beales
Choreographer	Andrew Panton
Video Artist	John Alder
Voice and Dialect Coach	Ros Steen
Assistant Director	Suzanne Graham
Stage Manager	Lee Davis
Deputy Stage Manager	Gemma Smith
Assistant Stage Manager	Hazel Price
Wardrobe Supervisor	Aileen Sherry

**First performed at the Traverse Theatre,
Friday 5 May 2006**

A Traverse Theatre Commission

TRAVERSE THEATRE

Artistic Director Philip Howard

Powerhouse of new writing. (Daily Telegraph)

The Traverse's commissioning process embraces a spirit of innovation and risk-taking that has launched the careers of many of Scotland's best-known writers including John Byrne, David Greig and David Harrower. It is unique in Scotland in that it fulfils the crucial role of providing the infrastructure, professional support and expertise to ensure the development of a dynamic theatre culture for Scotland.

The importance of the Traverse is difficult to overestimate...without the theatre, it is difficult to imagine Scottish playwriting at all. (Sunday Times)

From its conception in the 1960s, the Traverse has remained a pivotal venue during the Edinburgh Festival. It receives enormous critical and audience acclaim for its programming, as well as regularly winning awards. In 2001, the hugely successful *Gagarin Way* by Gregory Burke won Fringe First and Herald Angel awards. This was also the year the Traverse received a Herald Archangel Award for overall artistic excellence. In 2002, the Traverse produced award-winning shows, *Outlying Islands* by David Greig and *Iron* by Rona Munro and in 2003, *The People Next Door* by Henry Adam won Fringe First and Herald Angel Awards. In 2004, the Traverse produced the award-winning *Shimmer* by Linda McLean and a stage adaptation of Raja Shehadeh's diary account of the Israeli occupation of Ramallah, *When the Bulbul Stopped Singing*. The Traverse's 2005 programme received a record total of 12 awards, including a Fringe First for its own production, *East Coast Chicken Supper* by Martin J Taylor.

One of Europe's most important homes for new plays.
(Sunday Herald)

The Traverse's success isn't limited to either the Edinburgh stage or the Festival. Since 2001, *Gagarin Way, Outlying Islands, Iron, The People Next Door, When the Bulbul Stopped Singing*, the *Slab Boys Trilogy*, *Mr Placebo* and *Helmet* have toured not only within Scotland and the UK, but in Sweden, Norway, the Balkans, Germany, USA, Iran and Canada.

Auld Reekie's most important theatre. (The Times)

Now in its 14th year, the Traverse's annual Highlands & Islands tour is a crucial strand of our work. This commitment to Scottish touring has taken plays from our Edinburgh home to audiences all over Scotland. The Traverse has criss-crossed the nation performing at many diverse locations from Shetland to Dumfries, Aberdeen to Benbecula. The Traverse's 2005 production *I was a Beautiful Day* was commissioned to open the new An Lanntair Arts Centre in Stornoway, Isle of Lewis.

The Traverse Theatre has established itself as Scotland's leading exponent of new writing, with a reputation that extends worldwide. (The Scotsman)

The Traverse's work with young people is of supreme importance and takes the form of encouraging playwriting through its flagship education project *Class Act*, as well as the Young Writers' Group. *Class Act* is now in its 16th year and gives pupils the opportunity to develop their plays with professional playwrights and work with directors and actors to see the finished piece performed on stage at the Traverse. For the third year running, the project will also take place in Russia. In 2004 *Articulate*, a large scale project based on the *Class Act* model, took place in West Dunbartonshire working with 11 to 14 year olds. The hugely successful Young Writers' Group is open to new writers aged between 15 and 25 and the fortnightly meetings are led by a professional playwright.

The Traverse has an unrivalled reputation for producing contemporary theatre of the highest quality, invention and energy, and for its dedication to new writing. (Scotland on Sunday)

The Traverse is committed to working with international playwrights and in 2005 produced *In the Bag* by Wang Xiaoli in a version by Ronan O'Donnell, the first ever full production of a contemporary Chinese play in the UK. This project was part of the successful Playwrights in Partnership scheme, which unites international and Scottish writers, and brings the most dynamic new global voices to the Edinburgh stage. Other international Traverse partnerships have included work in Québec, Norway, Finland, France, Italy, Portugal and Japan.

www.traverse.co.uk

To find out about way in which you can support the work of the Traverse please contact Ruth Allan or Vikki Graves 0131 228 3223 or development@traverse.co.uk

Charity No. SC002368

COMPANY BIOGRAPHIES

John Alder (Video Artist)
John is an award-winning composer and film maker/editor. Stage credits include *Foreign Lands, A Clockwork Orange* (first and second production), *Edmond, 1984, Wings of Desire, Geneva, Frank, Tiger's Bride, Great Expectations* (Northern Stage); *Out of Nothing* (Northern Stage/Styx Theatre); *City of Sonnets* (Northern Stage/Title Productions); *One Day 49* (Styx Theatre); *Macbeth* (New College Theatre, Durham). John has worked extensively for television, composing music for various companies including BBC 1, BBC 2 and Channel 4. His video and music work has toured the UK, France, Holland and Finland.

Jon Beales (Composer)
Jon works extensively in theatre as a composer, musical director and sound designer. For the Traverse: *Wormwood, The Speculator* (Grec Festival, Barcelona/Edinburgh International Festival), *Solemn Mass for a Full Moon in Summer* (Traverse/Barbican). Other theatre credits include *Laurel & Hardy, A Christmas Carol, Guys & Dolls, Mother Courage* (Royal Lyceum Theatre, Edinburgh); *Into The Woods, The Secret Garden, Honk!, Masterclass* (Byre Theatre); *Kissing Angels* (National Youth Theatre); *The Tempest, Feelgood, Travesties, Mary Rose, Dear Brutus* and *A Midsummer Night's Dream* (Nottingham Playhouse); *Flora the Red Menace* (Dundee Rep); *Oliver!* (Perth Theatre); *Cat on a Hot Tin Roof* (Nottingham/Coventry/Edinburgh); *The Grapes of Wrath* (7:84); *The 39 Steps, Time and the Conways, Travels with my Aunt* (national tours). Film credits include *The Audition, The Total Eclipse of Sybil Price, I Got You, Deadbeat* and *Wasteland*.

Kai Fischer (Lighting Designer)
Kai studied Audio-Visual Media at the HDM in Stuttgart. For the Traverse: *I was a Beautiful Day, One Day All This Will Come to Nothing*. Other lighting design credits include *Endgame, The Dance of Death* (Citizens' Theatre); *Begin Again* (KtC), *The Wizard of Oz* (macrobert); *Merlin, The Danny Crowe Show* (Dundee Rep); *Great Expectations, Sleeping Beauty, Phedre* (Perth Theatre); *Woyzeck, Blood and Ice* (Royal Lyceum Theatre, Edinburgh); *Marching On* (7:84); *Switchback* (SweetScar); *Stroma* (TAG Theatre Company); *Macbeth, A Doll's House, Thebans, Uncle Vanya, Medea, Greeks* (Theatre Babel); *Beauty and the Beast* (Tron Theatre). Set and lighting designs include *Home - Caithness* (NTS); *Lost Ones, Stars Beneath the Sea, Invisible Man, A Brief History of Time, Last Stand* (Vanishing Point).

Suzanne Graham (Assistant Director)

Suzanne joined the Traverse in 2004 as Literary Development Officer. Her work for the Traverse has included co-ordinating the theatre's flagship education project *Class Act* both in Scotland and Russia, managing pilot projects *Articulate* (with West Dunbartonshire Council) and *Westside Stories* (with WHALE Learning Centre). She also co-ordinates the Young Writers' Group and related development projects.

Patrick Hoffman (*Dan*)

Patrick trained at Bretton Hall College. He has worked extensively with Foolsyard Theatre and Northern Stage over the past five years including tours of *1984* and *A Clockwork Orange*. He also participated in the making of *See-Saw*, an experimental project for Quarantine Theatre directed by Richard Gregory. Other theatre work includes two national tours with Fecund Theatre, *The Secret Agent* (Theatre Objektiv); *Project B* (The Works). Film credits include *Psyched Out* (Pilgrim Film); *Mrs Buchan* (Ipso Facto Film). Radio credits include two radio plays for BBC Radio 4.

Jules Horne (Writer)

Jules was born in Hawick and is currently Scottish Arts Council Virtual Writing Fellow in Dumfries & Galloway. Writing for radio includes *Left at the Lights* (BBC Radio Scotland); *Inner Critic* (BBC 7). Jules was awarded the National Library of Scotland Robert Louis Stevenson Memorial Award in 2002 and a Scottish Arts Council New Writer's Bursary in 2001. Her future projects include *A Place in the Rain* (BBC Radio 4) and *Overdue South* (CBL/Traverse/BBC Radio Scotland). *Gorgeous Avatar* is her first full-length theatre commission and was developed by the Traverse with the Scottish Book Trust's Mentoring Scheme.

Philip Howard (Director)

Philip trained under Max Stafford-Clark at the Royal Court Theatre, London, on the Regional Theatre Young Director Scheme from 1988-1990. Associate Director at the Traverse from 1993-1996, and Artistic Director since 1996. Productions at the Traverse include 18 world premieres of plays by David Greig, David Harrower, Catherine Czerkawska, Catherine Grosvenor, Ronan O'Donnell, Nicola McCartney, Linda McLean, Sue Glover, Iain Heggie, Iain F MacLeod and the late Iain Crichton Smith. Fringe First awards for *Kill the Old Torture Their Young, Wiping My Mother's Arse* and *Outlying Islands*. Other productions at the Traverse include *Faith Healer* by Brian Friel, *The Trestle at Pope Lick Creek* by Naomi Wallace, *Cuttin' a Rug* by John Byrne, *When the Bulbul Stopped Singing* by Raja Shehadeh (also Fadjr International Festival, Tehran; Off-Broadway, New York) and, as Co-Director, *Solemn Mass for a Full Moon in Summer* by Michel Tremblay (Traverse/Barbican). Productions elsewhere include *Words of Advice for Young People* by Ioanna Anderson (Rough Magic, Dublin), *The Speculator* by David Greig in Catalan (Grec Festival, Barcelona/ Edinburgh International Festival), *Entertaining Mr Sloane* (Royal, Northampton) and *Something About Us* (Lyric Hammersmith Studio). Radio credits include: *Being Norwegian* by David Greig (BBC Radio Scotland); *The Room* by Paul Brennen (BBC Radio 4)

John Kazek (*Rafi*)

John trained at RSAMD. For the Traverse: *I was a Beautiful Day,* the *Slab Boys Trilogy, Solemn Mass for a Full Moon in Summer* (Traverse/ Barbican), *King of the Fields, Perfect Days* (Traverse/Vaudeville), *Passing Places, Chic Nerds, Stones and Ashes, Europe.* Other theatre credits include *Roam* (Grid Iron/NTS); *1974 – The End of the Year Show* (Lyric Theatre, Belfast); *Knives in Hens* (TAG Theatre Company); *Hedda Gabler, Macbeth, Thebans, Uncle Vanya, 'Tis a Pity She's a Whore* (Theatre Babel); *Word for Word* (Magnetic North); *Pleasure and Pain, Glue, A Midsummer Night's Dream* (Citizens' Theatre); *Marabou Stork Nightmare* (Citizens' Theatre/Leicester Haymarket Theatre); *Variety* (Grid Iron); *The Big Funk* (The Arches); *Penetrator* (Tron Theatre); *Mary Queen of Scots, Kidnapped* (Royal Lyceum Theatre, Edinburgh); *Twilight Shift* (7:84); *Wuthering Heights, Driving Miss Daisy* (Byre Theatre); *King Lear, As You Like It* (Oxford Stage Company). Television credits include *The Key* (BBC/Little Bird); *Auf Wiedersehen Pet, City Central, Double Nougat, Rab C Nesbitt, Punch Drunk, Strathblair* (BBC); *Taggart, High Road* (STV). Film credits include *Batman Begins* (Warner Bros); *Dear Frankie* (Scorpio Films Ltd); *How D'Yae Want tae Die* (Dead Man's Shoes Ltd); *Young Adam* (Hanway Films); *Riff Raff* (Parallax Pictures); *Silent Scream* (Antonine Productions).

Pauline Knowles (*Amy*)

For the Traverse: *Heritage, The Trestle at Pope Lick Creek, Solemn Mass for a Full Moon in Summer* (Traverse/Barbican), *The Speculator* (Grec Festival, Barcelona/Edinburgh International Festival), *Widows, Knives in Hens, The Collection* and *Marisol.* Other theatre credits include *Macbeth, A Doll's House, Medea, King Lear* (Theatre Babel); *The White Cliff* (Oran Mor); *Martha* (Catherine Wheels Theatre Company); *Hey, Hey Good Looking* (Soho Theatre); *Vassa* (Albery Theatre/Almeida Theatre); *Othello, Men Should Weep, A Scots Quair* (TAG Theatre Company); *Swing Hammer Swing* (Citizens' Theatre); *Shining Souls* (Old Vic); *Twelfth Night* (Salisbury Theatre). Television credits include *Taggart* (STV); *Acting, Strathblair* (BBC); *John Brown's Body* (Channel 4); *Manhunters* (BBC 2). Radio credits include *Taglines, Subutu Passage, Floating, Wanting a Hand* (BBC).

Mark Leese (Designer)
For the Traverse: *The Ballad of Crazy Paola, Among Unbroken Hearts, Shetland Saga, The Speculator* (Grec Festival, Barcelona/Edinburgh International Festival), *Kill the Old Torture Their Young, Knives in Hens, Chic Nerds, Greta, Anna Weiss, Faith Healer, The Hope Slide* and *Brothers of Thunder*. Other theatre credits include *Shopping for Shoes, Prince Unleashed, The Pearl, Beethoven's Brother, Peacemaker, Bill's New Frock, Alfreda Abbot's Lost Voice, Hidden Lands, Pinocchio* (Visible Fictions) *Frogs* (Royal National Theatre); *Martin Yesterday* (Royal Exchange Theatre, Manchester); *Born Guilty, The War in Heaven, The Grapes of Wrath, Salt Wound, Antigone* (7:84); *On Golden Pond* (Royal Lyceum Theatre, Edinburgh). Film credits include *The Magdalene Sisters, Wilbur Wants to Kill Himself, Blinded, Things to Do Before You're 30, Woman in Winter, This is England*. Television credits include *The Book Group*.

Andrew Panton (Choreographer)
Andrew trained at the RSAMD (MDra Directing) and the Arts Educational Schools. He was the winner of the 2003 Bruce Millar Drama Award for emerging directors. Directing credits include *The Frog Prince* (Cardiff International Festival); *The Yellow on the Broom* (Perth Theatre); *Annie Get Your Gun* (Resident Director, National Tour); *Thumbelina, The Ten Magic Bridges, Around the World with Billy Brite* (Stephen Joseph Theatre); *Snake in the Grass* (Assistant Director, UK Tour); *Spittin' Distance, The Beginner's Guide to Cyber-shopping* (Associate Director/Musical Director, Stephen Joseph Theatre); *Stars Beneath the Sea* (Vanishing Point); *Halflife* (Tron Theatre); *Ubu the King* (Assistant Director, Arches Theatre). Workshop productions of new work for the RSAMD include *The Theory of the Leisure Class, Face 2 Face* and *Yeti*. Previous work as a choreographer includes *Magnitude* (Edinburgh Fringe Festival/tour); *Aladdin* (Perth Theatre); *Much Ado About Nothing* (Glasgow Repertory Theatre); *Something's Coming, Singin' & Swingin'* (Edinburgh Festival Theatre)

Una McLean (*Rose*)
Una trained at RSAMD. For the Traverse: *Melody, Shimmer,* the *Slab Boys Trilogy, Family, The Architect, Sky Woman Falling, Blending In, Ines de Castro*. Other theatre includes *The Kerry Matchmaker, Oklahoma, Annie* (Perth Theatre); *The Vagina Monologues* (Edinburgh Festival Theatre/Theatre Royal Glasgow); *Five Blue Haired Ladies Sitting on a Park Bench* (National tour, Brian Hewitt-Jones); *Beauty Queen of Leenane, Paddy's Market* (Tron Theatre); *Perfect Days* (Borderline Theatre Company); *Albertine in Five Times* (Clyde Unity Theatre); *Lovers, The Steamie* (Royal Lyceum Theatre, Edinburgh); *Mrs Warren and a Passionate Woman* (Pitlochry Festival Theatre);

Bourgeois Gentilhomme (Dundee Rep); *Couples* (Cacciatore Fabbro Prods, Edinburgh Festival); *Revolting Peasants* (7:84); *Beggar's Opera, Fiddler on the Roof* (Scottish Opera). She has played pantomimes for 25 consecutive years including *Cinderella, Snow White, Aladdin* and *Babes in the Wood*. Television work includes her own show *Did you see Una?* and the children's series *Captain Bonny*. Scottish Television profiled Una in an hour-long *Artery* special, *Numero Una*. Film work includes *Strictly Sinatra* (Universal Focus); *Nan* (Scottish Screen); *The Debt Collector* (Film Four/Pine Film); *Small Moments* (The Short Film Factory). Una was awarded a Doctorate of Letters in 1995 from Edinburgh's Queen Margaret College and an MBE in 2006.

Ros Steen (Voice and Dialect Coach)

Ros trained at RSAMD and has worked extensively in theatre, film and TV. For the Traverse: *Melody, I was a Beautiful Day, East Coast Chicken Supper, In the Bag,* the *Slab Boys Trilogy, Dark Earth, Homers, Outlying Islands, The Ballad of Crazy Paola, The Trestle at Pope Lick Creek, Heritage* (2001 and 1998), *Among Unbroken Hearts, Shetland Saga, Solemn Mass for a Full Moon in Summer* (as co-director, Traverse/ Barbican), *King of the Fields, Highland Shorts, Family, Kill the Old Torture Their Young, Chic Nerds, Greta, Lazybed, Knives in Hens, Passing Places, Bondagers, Road to Nirvana, Sharp Shorts, Marisol, Grace in America.* Other theatre credits include *Mystery of the Rose Bouquet, A Handful of Dust, Cleo, Camping, Emanuelle and Dick, A Whistle in the Dark, A Little Bit of Ruff* (Citizens' Theatre); *The Graduate, A Lie of the Mind, Macbeth, Twelfth Night, Dancing at Lugnasa* (Dundee Rep); *The Wonderful World of Dissocia* (Edinburgh International Festival/Drum Theatre Plymouth/Tron Theatre); *Uncle Varick, Playboy of the Western World* (Royal Lyceum Theatre, Edinburgh); *The Small Things* (Paines Plough); *Mancub* (Vanishing Point). Film credits include *Greyfriars Bobby* (Piccadilly Pictures); *Gregory's Two Girls* (Channel Four Films). Television credits include *Sea of Souls, 2000 Acres of Sky, Monarch of the Glen, Hamish Macbeth* (BBC).

SPONSORSHIP

Income from sponsorship enables the Traverse
to commission and produce new plays and offer
a diverse and exciting programme of events
throughout the year.

To find out more, please contact
Ruth Allan or Vikki Graves
0131 228 3223 or development@traverse.co.uk

We would like to thank the following
corporate sponsors for their support

  **B B C** Scotland

 STEWARTS

 ARCAS

 SCOTTISH BREWERS

 BIGGART BAILLIE

 BAIRDS
fine and country wines

HBJ Gateley Wareing  smg
tv productions

 LUMISON  KPMG

 NICHOLAS
GROVES
RAINES
ARCHITECTS

Willis

With thanks to

Claire Aitken of Royal Bank of Scotland for mentoring support arranged through the Arts & Business Mentoring Scheme.

Purchase of the Traverse Box Office, computer network and technical and training equipment has been made possible with money from The Scottish Arts Council National Lottery Fund.

LOTTERY FUNDED

The Traverse Theatre's work
would not be possible without the support of

The Traverse receives financial assistance from

The Calouste Gulbenkian Foundation,
The Peggy Ramsay Foundation, The Binks Trust,
The Wellcome Trust, Gouvernement de Québec,
The Canadian High Commission, The Japan Foundation,
The British Council

Sets, props and costumes for
Gorgeous Avatar
created by Traverse Workshops
(funded by the National Lottery)

Production photography by Douglas Robertson
Print photography by Euan Myles

ARE YOU DEVOTED?

Our Devotees are: Katie Bradford, Adrienne Sinclair Chalmers, Michael Ridings

The Traverse could not function without the generous support of our patrons. In March 2006 the Traverse Devotees was launched to offer a whole host of exclusive benefits to our loyal supporters.

Become a Traverse Devotee for £28 per month or £350 per annum and receive:

- A night at the theatre including six tickets, drinks and a backstage tour
- Your name inscribed on a brick in our wall
- Sponsorship of one of our brand new Traverse 2 seats
- Invitations to Devotees' events
- Your name featured on this page in Traverse Theatre Company scripts and a copy mailed to you
- Free hire of the Traverse Bar Café (subject to availability)

Bricks in our wall and seats in Traverse 2 are also available separately.

To join the Devotees or to discuss giving us your support in another way, please contact Ruth Allan or Vikki Graves on 0131 228 3223 or development@traverse.co.uk

For their continued generous support of Traverse productions, the Traverse thanks
Habitat; Marks and Spencer, Princes Street;
Camerabase; BHS and Holmes Place.

For their help on *Gorgeous Avatar* the Traverse thanks
A1 TV Services, Tron Theatre and Citizens' Theatre

For their support and inspiration, Jules Horne would like to thank
Michael Scott, Dorothy Alexander, Ian Brotherhood, Tom Bryan, Andrew Forster, Elspeth Smellie, Grahame Thomson, the Scottish Book Trust, everyone at the Traverse and especially Philip Howard.

TRAVERSE THEATRE – THE COMPANY

Ruth Allan	Development Associate
Aaron Butler	Second Chef
Lorne Campbell	Associate Director
Andy Catlin	Marketing Manager
Laura Collier	Artistic Administrator
David Connell	Finance Manager
Jason Cowing	Bar Café Executive Manager
Jennifer Cummins	Front of House Manager
Maureen Deacon	Finance Assistant
Martin Duffield	Box Office Manager
Anne Gallacher	Clore Leadership Fellow
Suzanne Graham	Literary Development Officer
Hannah Graves	Head Chef
Vikki Graves	Development Officer
Mike Griffiths	Administrative Director
Gavin Harding	Production Manager
Philip Howard	Artistic Director
Natalie Ibu	Marketing & Press Assistant
Aimee Johnstone	Bar Café Duty Manager
Kath Lowe	Deputy Front of House Manager
Norman Macleod	Development Manager
Kevin McCune	Senior Bar Café Duty Manager
Euan McLaren	Deputy Electrician
Katherine Mendelsohn	Literary Manager
Sarah Murray	Administrative Assistant
Dave Overend	Literary Assistant
Emma Pirie	Press & Marketing Officer
Pauleen Rafferty	Finance & Personnel Assistant
Claire Ramsay	Assistant Electrician
Renny Robertson	Chief Electrician
Phil Turner	Technical Stage Manager
Alan Wilkins	Young Writers Group Leader

Also working for the Traverse

Alice Boyle, Amy Breckon, Doug Broadley, Jimmy Butcher, Colum Cameron, Jonathan Cleaver, Dan Dixon, Amy Drummond, Andrew Dunn, Julie Eveleigh, Anna Forde, Rebecca Gerrard, Jane Gore, Nadia Graham, Dawid Grudzinski, Linda Gunn, Robyn Hardy, Zophie Horsted, Neil Johnstone, Kate Leiper, Dane Lord, Heather Marshall, Ailsa McLaggan, Adam Millar, John Mitchell, Tom Nickson, Christie O'Carroll, Amanda Olson, Clare Padgett, Finlay Pretsell, Greg Sinclair, Corin Sluggett, Emma Taylor, Gillian Taylor, Ailsa Thomson, Matt Vale, Jenna Watt, Kris Wedlock, Camilla Wegener, Katie Wilson

TRAVERSE THEATRE BOARD OF DIRECTORS

Stephen Cotton (Chair), Chris Hannan, Christine Hamilton, Caroline Gardner, John Stone, Stuart Murray (Company Secretary), Margaret Waterston

GORGEOUS AVATAR

Jules Horne

For Michael Scott

Valentine by a Telegraph Clerk

The tendrils of my soul are twined
With thine, though many a mile apart,
And thine in close-coiled circuits wind
Around the needle of my heart.

Constant as Daniel, strong as Grove,
Ebullient throughout its depths like Smee,
My heart puts forth its tide of love,
And all its circuits close in thee.

O tell me, when along the line
From my full heart the message flows,
What currents are induced in thine?
One click from thee will end my woes.

Through many a volt the weber flew,
And clicked this answer back to me;
I am thy farad staunch and true,
Charged to a volt with love for thee.

James Clerk Maxwell, 1860

Characters

AMY, *woman, thirties*

DAN, *man, thirties*

ROSE, *woman, fifties*

RAFI, *man, thirties*

Sentences without full stops are connected to later ones.

Slashes indicate / interruption or synchronicity.

Round brackets reflect (interiority).

Chevron brackets represent <internet exchanges>.

This text went to press before the end of rehearsals so may differ slightly from the play as performed.

ACT ONE

Scene One

in which Amy doesn't panic

Early morning. A run-down cottage with a computer. A muddy space outside, a chopping log, an outhouse wall. Clutter of weeds and wood and plant pots and plastic. Autumn leaves tickle across the stage. Sound: quiet crows, sheep. A computer boots up and beeps. Smell: grass, woodsmoke. AMY *appears in T-shirt, tracksuit bottoms and cardigan. She puts on her wellies, goes outside for a couple of logs, returns and begins raking out the fire.* DAN *enters. He stretches each leg against the chopping log, scratches a furious itch. He listens at* AMY*'s door, almost knocks.* ROSE *enters, wearing paint-spattered tracksuit bottoms and a T-shirt. She lays out a dustsheet on the ground next to the outhouse wall. A low military jet screams suddenly overhead. They all look, listen and wait for the second jet, which doesn't come.*

ROSE. Morning!

DAN. Yeah. Morning.

> ROSE *leaves for her cottage.* DAN *leaves for his cottage.*
> AMY *clears out the fire.*

AMY. Then, you scrape the grate, like so. Down each groove, from top to bottom, moving gradually in an eastward direction. The wrist action should be smooth and firm. Take care not to miss any grooves. I like to use a brass poker, available from most good hardware stores. As you can see, the ash falls through the holes and lands conveniently in the ash pan, like so. What's left behind is known, technically speaking, as clinker. Derived from the French, clink-er. To clink. I clink, you clink, he she it clinks. Nous clinkons, vous clinkez, ils clinkent. Ecoutez, et repetez.

The second jet screams past. AMY *gets a fright. She knocks the ashpan. A cloud of ash.*

Deep breath. Always deep breath. (*She cleans.*) You have a choice. To open, or not to open. It is your door. After all, it's a busy day. Busy busy. Busybusybusy. On busy days like these, it's advisable to follow a to-do list. You can buy them ready-made, or simply make your own, using a sheet of standard A4. This will help you to prioritise. Step one: lay the fire. Step two: finish the Paris contract. Step two a: Start the Paris contract. Step two a one: Panic about not starting the Paris contract. Step three: God. 'S not a big deal. Hello and welcome. Good flight? Nice landing? Smooth? Welcome to my humble bath. He won't be using the bath. Will he be using the bath? Maybe it's polite to offer the bath. It's a long way to come. He'll maybe need a bath. He'll maybe need towels. Maybe a sleep. He can't have a sleep. No here. No in my place. Deep breath. Always deep breath. Break it into steps. Step four: faff around. Always faff around. (*To herself.*) I faff, you faff, he she it faffs, nous faffons, vous faffez –

DAN *enters.*

DAN. Ils faffent.

AMY. Christ.

DAN. I do it all the time.

AMY. I wasn't / talking to myself.

DAN. / Talking to yourself. It's OK.

AMY. I was practising.

DAN. Insanity?

AMY. French.

Scene Two

in which Amy and Dan discuss whether fate is a pro or a con

DAN. Have you got onto conversation yet? Cos that's when to really start worrying. Bonjour, monsieur. Bonjour, ça va? Tres bien, merci. Et vous? Absolument brilliant. And before you know it you've got Jean-Claude and Marie-France and the wee bébé and the whole gang of them blurting away at you. Somebody's been tidying.

AMY. It's no that unusual.

DAN. Making an effort.

AMY. So?

DAN (*insinuating*). So . . .

AMY. I dusted, OK?

DAN. So *so* . . .

AMY. The ash was

DAN. I know.

AMY. flying

DAN. 'letting you down'

AMY. all over the place

DAN. 'making a wrong impression'

AMY. It fair needed –

DAN. on any passers-by

AMY. Just dusting.

DAN. who might be

AMY. Just the mantelpiece.

DAN. passing by.

AMY. Your point is?

DAN. Why the effort?

AMY. Everybody dusts.

DAN. The *sudden* effort.

AMY. Because

DAN. The *today* effort.

AMY. Because today, for once, I don't want to look like someone who doesn't make an effort.

AMY sits at the computer and tries to work.

DAN. When's he due?

AMY. Shortly.

Pause.

DAN. You'll be taking him out.

AMY. Maybe.

DAN. He's come all this way.

AMY. His choice.

DAN. Show him some things. The sights. Get yourself out the place.

AMY. He's come all this way to be *here,* no out there gallivanting. Just to meet. Say hello. Cup of tea. Out the door.

DAN. S'a nice top.

AMY. (He can see his own sights.)

DAN. That new?

AMY. (He'll have a car.)

DAN. I saw the postie with a boxie.

AMY. (He'll have his own plans.)

DAN. S'a nice top for just a cup of tea.

AMY. A girl can't have a nice top?

DAN. You should go for a walk. Serious. (*Off* AMY*'s look.*) You should try it sometime, going for a walk. There's all this green stuff growing. Birds belting their wee hearts out. See what I saw yesterday? A salmon. Up and out the water and arching and plopping back in there like a big fat stone. I've never seen that before. Usually they do it just out of sight to piss you off. And there it was. My personal own dedicated salmon. The clichéd wee bastard. A leaping salmon, for chrissake. I thought it was just a phrase. But they really do that stuff. I stood there half an hour. Never showed his face again. Holding his breath, he was, swimming all the way up, gasping, hiding under rocks. 'You think I'm coming up again, don't you?' A slimy wee fish smile on him. You'd like it. Getting out the place.

AMY. Just because I don't have a brass plaque on the door, doesn't mean I'm no working. I've no your time.

DAN. We've all the same time.

AMY. No.

DAN. Twenty-four hours free with every day.

AMY *stops trying to work.*

AMY. Have you taken your pill?

DAN. No.

AMY. You should take your pill.

DAN. I'm good.

AMY. Cos I can't –

DAN. It's OK.

AMY. – spend –

DAN. Fine.

AMY. – time –

DAN. I'm doing stuff.

AMY. – Not today.

DAN. I'm helping Rose with her video.

AMY. She know that?

DAN. She asked me.

AMY. There's a first.

DAN. We're doing the video diary. A heart-warming tale of a run-down shack, and how it turns its life around, becomes a gleaming palace, meets a rich buyer, and Rose lives happily ever after.

AMY (*trying to type*). (. . . stunning . . .)

DAN. Thing is, because it's a makeover show, we need somewhere to play the run-down shack.

AMY. (. . . stunning . . .)

DAN. We thought maybe here.

AMY. (. . . stunning . . .)

DAN. Are you listening?

AMY. What's another word for stunning?

DAN. Gorgeous.

AMY. I've used gorgeous.

DAN. Amazing.

AMY. Got that.

DAN. Beautiful.

AMY. More than beautiful.

DAN. Gobsmacking.

AMY. The wrong tone.

DAN. Jaw-dropping.

AMY. Too OTT.

DAN. Fantabulous.

AMY. A *real* word.

DAN. It's a real word.

AMY. It doesn't exist.

DAN. It does now.

AMY. Aye.

DAN. What's wrong with stunning? If it does the job.

AMY. I've used it that many times. For everything. For boats and weather and views and wee cropped jackets with decorative piping and I'm sick of it. It's gone flat on me.

DAN. Maybe you've gone flat on *it*. Maybe you need to go out and be stunned now and then. It's hard to keep being stunned by the same four walls.

The phone rings. AMY *types at the computer, ignores the phone.*

Want me to get that?

AMY. You dare.

The answerphone kicks in. They listen to the message and speak over it.

AMY'S VOICE. Hello. You're through to Wordsworth. All our lines . . .

DAN (*over*). / All our lines?

AMY'S VOICE. / . . . are busy at the moment. I'm sorry we can't take your call, but please leave a message and we'll get back to you.

Answerphone beep. AMY *freezes.*

DAN. Who's we?

AMY. Shh.

DAN. / You and your invisible pal?

AMY. . . .

DAN. Or is it the the royal 'we'?

AMY. !

DAN. He can't hear.

LIEVRE'S VOICE (*under*). / Allo? This is Michel Lièvre, with a message for Mme McAllister, we are still awaiting your file, we need it urgently, please to get in touch, thank you.

A silence. The call ends.

AMY. He knows I'm here. (*Typing.*) (a – stunning – building)

DAN. How can he know?

AMY. He can tell. (*Typing.*) (magnificent – building)

DAN. He can't.

AMY. He heard you. (*Typing.*) (magnificent – *complex*)

DAN. No way.

AMY. – *outstanding* – complex –

DAN. Somebody's getting edgy.

AMY. – *striking* complex –

DAN. Somebody's getting

AMY (*shouts*). *Stunning* complex.

DAN. – excited.

AMY. A bit.

DAN. I'm jealous.

AMY. Aye, right.

   DAN*'s mind is elsewhere in the room.*

DAN. I mean, how did he pull it off? Technically. The tricks. What's he got that I haven't got?

AMY. Mystery.

DAN. I can do mystery. See, what you don't know about me is . . . I'm really a . . . a Russian count, down on his luck, very down on his luck, hole in T-shirt, see, but worth millions – of roubles – which isn't much, given the state of the rouble, but . . .

AMY (*typing*). And what's brought you here?

DAN. Sanctuary.

   AMY *stops typing.*

AMY. You feeling OK?

DAN. Fantabulous.

AMY. Did you sleep?

DAN. No.

AMY. The owls.

DAN. . . . the trees. The grass growing. It grows fucking loud.

AMY. You could shut the window.

DAN. I did. But there was this bloke breathing. Wheezing like a deep-sea diver. All night.

AMY. You.

DAN. Yeah. He kept me awake. Bloody inconsiderate.

AMY (*re* DAN*'s shiftiness*). There's no point in looking.

DAN. I'm not looking.

AMY. You're looking all the time.

DAN. I'm fine.

   AMY *fishes car keys from a hiding place.*

AMY. Here.

DAN. No.

AMY. Away you go.

DAN. There's no petrol in it.

AMY. I'll stand you the money.

DAN. I don't want the money.

AMY. So stop looking.

DAN. I'm not / looking.

AMY. / You're looking all the time, Dan. Every time you're *in* here, / you're looking.

DAN. / What's wrong?

AMY. With *me*?

DAN. Sorry.

AMY. I'm hiding things. I'm hiding things in my own house. (*Re the keys.*) Go on.

DAN. I don't want them.

AMY. Neither do I.

DAN *takes the keys.*

DAN. See, what I worry about with you is: you trust people. You think they're basically good. And they're not. They're basically not.

AMY. I'm learning.

DAN. You're not. Cos you've got some guy coming –

AMY. He's not 'some guy'.

DAN. Who is he then?

AMY. A friend.

DAN. You hardly know him.

AMY. I know him enough.

DAN. Through email?

AMY. Yeah.

DAN. Words?

AMY. Yeah.

Pause.

DAN. Say you saw this guy at the station. All the people, running around. Strangers. Don't-know-from-bloody-Adams. Would you go up and talk to him?

AMY. (Maybe.)

DAN. Would you go up and grab him by the collar and tell him about yourself? Here's my heart and here's my sleeve and look, there it is, throbbing away like a sweet-going motor.

AMY. Come on.

DAN. I'm not trying to panic you –

AMY. You're doing OK.

DAN. *But –*

AMY. He might be a nutter.

DAN. He might.

AMY. He isn't.

DAN. How do you know?

AMY. He can spell.

They smile. Pause.

It's an adventure. You're always telling me to have an adventure.

DAN. I meant go shopping.

AMY. Got to start somewhere.

DAN. I'll be keeping an eye out.

AMY. No curtain-twitching.

DAN. Just an eye.

AMY. No coming to borrow stuff.

DAN. Stuff runs out.

AMY. You dare.

DAN. He might have an axe.

AMY. *I've* got an axe.

Scene Three

in which Rose rejects romance in favour of practicalities

ROSE *enters with a camcorder.*

ROSE. And before you start –

DAN. I haven't started.

ROSE. You're going to start.

DAN. I'm not starting.

ROSE. You always do.

DAN (*to* AMY). Am I starting?

ROSE. Don't you start.

DAN. I haven't even started starting.

ROSE. See? There he goes.

> ROSE *gives the camcorder to* DAN, *who gets it working.*

DAN. She loves me really.

ROSE. I liked you better in your nappies. The wee holiday
  boy, greeting in my mother's nettles every summer. And her
  scraping her pension to keep you in sweeties. (*To* AMY.)
  The parents never bought sweeties. Bad for you. Like a
  baggie net was bad for you cos you might drown in the
  burn, and a bogey was bad for you cos you might skin your
  knees, and bad boys were bad for you cos they might have
  baggie nets and bogeys and make you eat berries and be
  sick and die. Some holiday. (*Re* DAN.) He's keeping you
  back.

AMY. No more than usual.

ROSE (*to* DAN). Shame on you. She's a working girl. Unlike
  some folk I could mention.

DAN. Don't be fooled by all the kit. She only uses it for
  Solitaire.

ROSE. That's nice.

DAN. And online romance.

ROSE. Should get myself a computer.

DAN. For online romance?

ROSE. Sounds like the way to go about it. High tech, low
  maintenance.

DAN. They can still turn up on your doorstep.

ROSE. You'd hardly give them your address, would you? (*Off* DAN*'s look.*) She never.

AMY (*warning*). Dan.

ROSE. Is that this visitor?

AMY. No.

DAN. From the good ol' U of S.

ROSE. An American?

AMY. He's a friend.

ROSE. I hear they're mostly circumcised.

DAN. Your chance to find out.

AMY. He's my cousin.

ROSE. Which side?

AMY. The American side.

ROSE. Don't discount cousins. It's perfectly legal.

AMY. He's only coming for a coffee.

DAN. Kwawfee.

ROSE. He's fair keen on his coffee.

AMY. He's on a trip. I'm on his way.

ROSE. They fair get about, Americans. Can you tell him no to park in front of my window?

AMY. Whatever.

ROSE. I'm keeping that space for Jessica. My producer. Awful nice on the phone.

AMY. You found the camcorder.

ROSE. Under the ottoman. I mean to say. If they will make things that small.

DAN (*to* AMY). She hasn't started her video diary yet.

ROSE (*guilty*). Well . . .

DAN. A year's worth of diary.

ROSE. I've been busy. Turning that house inside out and
    backend foremost. Mother would be livid, the auld greeting-
    face. New wiring, new plaster, new doorbell, new carpets . . .
    Nothing left to girn about. Pity she's no here to see it. I'd
    love to hear her speechless. And her just a month off her
    telegram when she went. Typical. She'd have girned about
    that ana. (*Beat.*) Aye, it's a different place now.

DAN. That's your problem. You can't film an 'after' if you
    haven't got a 'before'.

ROSE. We'll use here.

AMY. No.

DAN. They'll never buy it.

ROSE. Somebody's got to buy it. My old age depends on it.

AMY. My house is not a 'before'.

DAN. It *is* a bit 'during'.

ROSE. It's before the invention of hoovers.

AMY. Out.

ROSE (*to* DAN). Come on, you. We need to get some footage
    in the cans.

    ROSE *and* DAN *leave.*

Scene Four

in which Amy and Rafi meet and greet

Inside the cottage. AMY *is at the computer.*

AMY (*typing*). A stunning – new building – in the heart of Paris.
    In the bustling heart – in the pulsating – in the *throbbing* –
    heart of Paris. Throbbing away like a sweet-going motor.
    Where tradition confronts modernity – where tradition
    meets modernity – where they meet for the very first –

A knock at the door: dddD. AMY *freezes.*

Another knock. AMY *rises.*

Who is it?

RAFI. It's me.

AMY. Hello.

RAFI. Is that you?

AMY. You?

RAFI. Amy?

AMY. That's me.

RAFI. Can I come in?

AMY. I –

RAFI. You got my message?

AMY. Yes. No –

RAFI. I can come back.

AMY. No. You're here.

RAFI. OK. (*Pause.*) This is strange.

AMY. Strange.

RAFI. OK. I'm cool.

AMY. I'm cool, too.

RAFI. Good.

AMY. Did you have a good flight?

RAFI. I did. / It

AMY. / You must be tired.

RAFI. Yes. It would be nice to kind of . . .

AMY. Yes?

RAFI. . . . sit down.

AMY. You want a / seat. . . .

RAFI. / chair, maybe?

AMY. . . . chair?

RAFI. There isn't a chair out here.

AMY. You'd better come in.

> RAFI *enters. He has a moustache.* AMY *has her back to him.*

RAFI. Hello.

AMY. Hello.

RAFI. Again.

AMY. You're welcome.

RAFI. I tried to buy flowers. I looked everywhere. I couldn't find anything suitable.

AMY. That's OK.

RAFI. Only small ones and mean ones or cellophane ones with wrapped-in smells. Nothing I'd call a flower aren't you going to turn round?

AMY. Yes.

RAFI. It makes communication somewhat / uneven.

AMY. / we talked about this.

RAFI. Yes.

AMY. Seeing each other.

RAFI. We did.

AMY. For the first time.

RAFI. Visually speaking.

AMY. How it'll change things.

RAFI. / Why?

AMY. / Between us.

RAFI. We've seen pictures.

AMY. They're not the same. They're not –

RAFI. Kinetic?

AMY. That's right.

RAFI. And they don't talk, I suppose.

AMY. Or smell of / aftershave.

RAFI. / Perfume. I should have brought flowers.

AMY. It might have helped.

RAFI. To bridge . . .

AMY. the / gap.

RAFI. / distance. Look at me.

AMY. Listen.

They listen. Quiet countryside. Birds.

This is where we are when we meet for the first time.

Pause.

RAFI. May I?

AMY. I think so.

RAFI moves closer.

RAFI. I can smell your hair.

AMY. I can feel your breath.

RAFI. Is it / mango?

AMY. / Peach.

They stand for a long moment.

RAFI. Turn round.

AMY turns round.

AMY. A moustache.

RAFI. Do you like it?

AMY. No. I mean yes.

RAFI. I haven't had it long.

AMY. Take it off.

RAFI. Are you sure?

AMY. Get rid of it.

RAFI. It's a good mustache. Luxuriant. Silky.

AMY. It's facial hair.

RAFI. It's a lot of work, a fine mustache like this. You have to tend it.

AMY. I know.

RAFI. Tweak it. Remove the wilful wiry ones. Keep it clean and sanitary.

AMY. It's got to go. It's not right.

RAFI. Doesn't it have something of the Clark Gable? Something debonair? Something old-world and / charming?

AMY. / You look like a spiv. A spiv on the hunt for a sucker. Before I know it you'll be selling me insurance.

RAFI. That's a shocking prejudice.

AMY. That's a shocking moustache.

RAFI (*warning*). Faces can look different suddenly, without hair. The mouth is revealed. It might not be the mouth you were expecting. It could be fuller or thinner or redder or wetter. It could be a different mouth entirely.

AMY. I don't care.

RAFI. I grew it for you.

AMY. I can never kiss you.

RAFI. No? Hell.

He tears off his moustache.

AMY. That's better. More like the picture.

RAFI. Where were we?

AMY. Almost touching.

RAFI. Almost.

AMY. Not quite.

> RAFI *moves closer.*

RAFI. Is this erotic for you?

AMY. Don't spoil it.

RAFI. But you've had those thoughts?

AMY. I have not had those thoughts.

RAFI. *I* have.

AMY. I don't want to know.

RAFI. And so have you.

AMY. They never crossed my mind.

RAFI. Then why am I here? Why have I come all this way? Just to look at you?

AMY. That's enough.

> RAFI *grabs* AMY.

RAFI. I've had those thoughts, I'm telling you. Want me to show you? Want me to make your blood run hot?

AMY. Let go!

> *They struggle.* AMY *elbows* RAFI *in the groin. He crumples.*

God. I didn't mean to. It was going fine. Going really well. Let's start again. Pretend it never happened.

> *The phone rings.* AMY *listens. The answerphone kicks in. The message is slightly different.*

AMY'S VOICE. Hello. You're through to Wordsworth. I'm sorry we can't take your call – all our operators are busy at the moment. But leave your number and we'll get back to you as soon as we can.

RAFI (*over*). You want me to leave?

AMY. Shh.

RAFI *limps off.*

LIEVRE'S VOICE (*French accent*). Allo. This is Michel Lièvre, Mme McAllister, we have not received your file. M. Stefanovic has arrived. We would like to hear from you. Thank you.

AMY *goes to the computer.*

AMY. An *exciting* new venue in the heart of Paris. A *magnificent* new venue in the . . . *exciting* heart of Paris. The *exciting* heart of . . . *magnificent* Paris. The *magnificent* heart of *outstanding* Paris. The *magnificent* heart . . . the magnificent heart . . .

AMY *likes this result. She continues typing at the computer.*

Scene Five

in which Rose films the winter of her discontent

ROSE *and* DAN *enter. DAN sets up the video camera on a tripod, looks around for an angle.*

ROSE. Heck. She's tidied up. All year it's been a midden and now she tidies up.

ROSE *moves planks, paint pots and rubbish to make a messy shot. She walks into shot.*

How's that?

DAN. Fantabulous.

ROSE. We'll go for a take. 'A Kick up the Market, Rose Guthrie, Take One.' December. Mind and say 'cut' at the end.

DAN. OK.

DAN *films. Pause.*

ROSE. And 'action' at the beginning.

DAN. Action.

ROSE (*misunderstanding*). Aye.

DAN. Action.

ROSE. Now?

DAN. Yes.

ROSE. Go on then.

DAN. Action!

ROSE. Brrrrr. It's December and I've just moved in. It's freezing. Brrrr. Even for December. Snow on the way, it said on the telly. There's planks and paint pots all over the place. Coming down wi paint pots. And planks. And DIY stuff. You can't get moving for DIY stuff. It's an absolute midden. I'm that depressed. Brrrr. I can't wait for the spring to arrive, when it'll be a wee bit warmer, and not so freezing as now, in the winter. Thank you.

DAN. So when's this Jessica due?

ROSE. Two.

DAN. And you've had this how long?

ROSE. Doesn't time fly?

DAN (*re the camera*). Ottoman bollocks. I saw this on the sideboard. It's been on the sideboard all year.

ROSE. I wanted to do it properly.

DAN. They don't want properly on DIY telly. They want mess and chaos and disaster. They want burst pipes and earthquakes and people having babies up ladders in a storm.

ROSE. They'll have to want. I've had a death to sort, and a house to do up.

DAN *finds a dead branch and places it in shot.*

What's that for?

DAN. It's a symbol.

ROSE. It's a dead branch.

DAN. You need to make an effort or they'll never believe it. You're underdressed for a start.

ROSE. They'd hardly expect me to grout in a tiara.

DAN. You need a jumper. A big coat.

ROSE. You're right. And a scarf. And a hat.

ROSE *leaves.*

DAN (*calls*). Lipstick.

DAN *lights a cigarette, fiddles with the tripod, arranges the mess, scratches.* ROSE *returns with thick clothes and boots. She puts them on.*

I've never been here in winter.

ROSE. You don't want to be.

DAN. But I only know it in the summer. I've never seen it freezing or flooded or up to its knees in snow. I've only seen the half of it.

ROSE. You wouldn't like the other half. You'd hate it. Power cuts and no hot water and heating cold beans in a pan on the grate. You'd be wall-to-wall girning and back to Gateshead first sight of a thaw. That's the trouble with you folk. All the smooth, none o the rough.

DAN. You about ready?

ROSE. That'll do me.

DAN. You're too neat.

ROSE. I've got to look my best.

DAN. You've got to look your worst. To get the full effect. Before and after.

ROSE. There's a limit to how 'before' I'm willing to go on primetime telly.

DAN *ruffles her hair, pinches her cheeks, messes her clothes.*

That'll do.

DAN. Are you ready to roll?

ROSE. We'll go for a take.

DAN. And . . . action.

Pause.

Take your time. I've got all year.

ROSE. It's gone.

DAN. Winter. Cold. Miserable.

ROSE. I'm thinking.

DAN. Everything in a state. Falling to bits. Empty shell.

ROSE. I'm trying to remember.

DAN. What was it like in the winter?

ROSE. It's no good.

DAN. You want to sell this house or not?

ROSE. I need a run at it.

DAN. Give me the lipstick.

DAN rubs lipstick on her nose and cheeks. As he speaks, he realigns the camera, positions the props.

Shut your eyes. Shut! Sit down. Face to me. Deep breath.

ROSE. OK.

DAN blows on her face.

DAN. Feel that?

ROSE. I can feel something.

DAN. The wind getting up.

ROSE. I can feel it on my cheek.

DAN. It's getting stronger. Shhh.

ROSE. From the north, it's coming.

A wind gets up. The lighting gradually turns wintry. Sound: a suggestion of winter. DAN underlines this with his own sounds effects.

DAN. Listen to the trees. Rustling. Shhhhh. Dry, they are. There's a big gust coming now. Shhhhhhh. It's tearing all the leaves off the trees. There they go, down and down, into the cold, wet mud.

ROSE. I'm getting it.

DAN. All the branches bare as antlers.

ROSE. Falling.

DAN. It's December.

ROSE. December.

DAN. It's cold.

ROSE. Cold.

DAN. It's windy.

ROSE. Wild . . .

DAN. It's damp, it's dark, it's / miserable.

ROSE. / Dreich . . .

DAN. You're in an empty room, the walls echoing.

ROSE. The upstairs bedroom . . .

DAN. Lying on the mattress, freezing in your sleeping bag, listening to the wind . . .

ROSE. howling in the stairwell . . .

DAN. You're shivering, you can't get to sleep, your eyes are watering, your nose is dripping . . .

ROSE. My arms are crippled from painting the hall . . .

DAN. And . . . ?

ROSE. The window's broken. The floorboards . . . ?

DAN. The floorboards are bare.

ROSE. The heating's off.

DAN. The toilet's blocked.

ROSE. The roof's leaking.

DAN. The phone's cut.

ROSE. The walls are / damp.

DAN. / wringing with / damp.

ROSE. / hinging with damp. It smells like an unfilled grave.

DAN (*quiet*). Go on . . .

ROSE. It's a hovel. A stinking hovel in the middle of beyond.
Who in their right mind takes on a wreck like this? I'll
never make it right. No all the tiling and slating and
screeding in the world willna make it right. No by her, the
miserable auld scunner.

Pause.

DAN (*quiet*). . . . and . . . / cut.

ROSE. / Could you no have made up your mind for once in
ninety-odd year? Stay with a will, or kick your clogs? Put
us all out our misery? I'd've done the place out years ago if
you'd let me in the door. Painted it up and got you upstairs
power and new units and a heater in the bedroom. You
didn't need to live like that. You auld martyr. Stoking up
your pennies to spend in heaven. I didn't want them. No if it
meant being grateful. Well, I've got them now. You've a
place fit to live in now. Like it or lump it. New floors and
curtains and sconces in the hall. Brass sconces. Cost a
bloody fortune. So. That'll do, eh?

DAN. That'll do.

ROSE. Spring now. I've some daffodils in the sideboard.

ROSE *leaves.* DAN *collapses the tripod, tidies the winter
props and follows her.*

Scene Six

in which Amy plays Solitaire, and consequences

AMY. Ten of hearts . . . nine of clubs. Eight of spades . . . seven of diamonds. Two of clubs . . . Damn. Deal again? No, back to work. Just a little one? Oh, go on, then. Just one more game.

Effects: a Solitaire hand is dealt by the computer.

'And what's your view, Dr McAllister, on the continuing fascination of Solitaire?' 'Well, Jeremy, expert studies have confirmed that it's entirely sexual.' 'Explain yourself, Dr McAllister.' 'Isn't it obvious, Jeremy? The long, gradual build-up, the slow approach towards the elusive prize, the almost, the almost . . . and the yes! The cards tumble, cascade, spill like a waterfall. Admit it, Jeremy. Can *you* settle to *work* until you've experienced that delicious release?'

ROSE *enters, bearing fake daffodils.*

ROSE. I wandered lonely as a cloud, daDAA daDAA daDAA daDAA, daDAA daDAA daDAA daDAA, diddly diddly in the breeze.

AMY. Fluttering.

ROSE. Sorry?

AMY. Fluttering and diddly in the breeze.

ROSE. Like yours truly after a night at The Queen's. (*Beat.*) He's no here yet, then? The prodigal cousin.

AMY. When I say 'cousin' . . .

ROSE. Aye?

AMY. He's more of a removed cousin.

ROSE. Twice removed?

AMY. At least.

ROSE. The more removed the better. You know what they say about close-knit genes.

A knock at the door.

DAN (*American accent*). Hello?

AMY. Oh!

ROSE. Oh!

AMY. What'll I do?

ROSE. Sort your hair.

AMY. Am I OK?

ROSE. You're fine. What about me?

AMY. Never mind you.

ROSE. Are you going to get that?

AMY. No.

ROSE. Do you want me to get that?

AMY. No!

ROSE. Don't panic.

AMY. I'm not!

Another knock at the door.

ROSE. Dear Lord.

DAN. Anybody home?

ROSE *gestures encouragingly to* AMY.

AMY (*calling*). Yes. Just a minute!

DAN (*calling*). Hello?

AMY. Hello!

Pause.

ROSE. Hello!

DAN. That you, Amy?

Pause.

AMY. Who is it?

DAN. I'm looking for Amy.

ROSE. Your cousin Amy?

DAN. That's the one.

AMY (*to* ROSE). You keep out of this.

ROSE. I'll away out the back door.

AMY. You're staying put.

ROSE. Make up your mind.

DAN. Do you know where she is? I believe she's expecting me.

ROSE. He sounds nice. Will I look out the window?

AMY. No.

ROSE. The upstairs bedroom?

AMY. Right. You're just leaving, OK? The minute I open the door, out you go.

ROSE. Fine.

AMY. No hovering.

ROSE. He'll be wanting a cup of tea, though.

AMY. And you won't. Is that clear?

ROSE. He's waiting.

AMY *opens the door.*

DAN. Well hello there, purty lady.

AMY. / Bastard.

ROSE. / Bizzum.

DAN. Mind if I just mosey right on in?

AMY. You got nothing better to do?

ROSE. You had us there.

DAN. Well doggone, if it ain't the cutest little home I ever did see.

AMY *fumes.*

ROSE. Fair up to high doh, we were.

AMY *sits at the computer.*

DAN. Let's leave it.

ROSE. We'll be quick.

DAN. Maybe we'd better / do it outside.

ROSE. / It's fine.

DAN. Where do you want to be?

ROSE. In front of the mould. The wall's hinging with it. Can we move the settee?

AMY *doesn't answer. She types. They move the settee.*

Chhh.

DAN (*to* AMY). Lighten up.

AMY. (This magnificent building)

ROSE. What a state.

DAN. I was just

ROSE. It's the worst it's been.

AMY. (in the heart of Paris . . .)

DAN. having a laugh.

ROSE. It's spread – look. It's onto the skirting.

AMY. (This *outstanding* building . . .)

DAN. A laugh.

ROSE. There's a bit on the settee. You want to watch that.

AMY. (This outstanding, magnificent, stunning building . . .)

DAN. OK?

ROSE. It can get into your lungs. You want to air the place more.

ROSE *opens the door wide. Papers rustle.*

AMY. No!

ROSE. We're in the way.

AMY. You're in my house.

ROSE (*re the sofa*). Should I move it back?

AMY. Give me that.

AMY *takes the camera.*

DAN. Sorry.

AMY. Come on.

DAN. But –

AMY. The red button?

DAN. Yes.

AMY. Just press it?

DAN. Whatever.

AMY. Go on. Do your thing.

ROSE. I don't know.

AMY. What don't you know?

ROSE. Where should I . . . ?

AMY. Down a bit. With your back to the mould.

ROSE. I'll get it on my / clothes.

AMY. / It'll wash off. (*Pause.*) OK.

ROSE (*re the camera*). Is that you . . . ?

AMY. Running.

DAN. She needs to / get into

ROSE. / I need to work up to it.

AMY. Go on, then.

ROSE. I need to think.

AMY. I haven't got all day.

ROSE. I can't remember the spring.

AMY *films* ROSE.

AMY. It was wet. Wet and cold.

ROSE. Wet . . . ?

DAN *hands* ROSE *a raincoat. Gradually, the light changes. A wind gets up.*

AMY. Wet and cold. Not *still* and cold. *Windy* and cold. Things are moving. The sky heavy. The wet waiting

ROSE. To soak you through. Your mood. Your bones. Through the pointing and into the wall.

DAN *hands* ROSE *an umbrella. She reacts to the swelling wind.* DAN *climbs on a chair with a watering can.*

AMY. The rain clouds are moving from all directions. All the clouds in the country. Banking up in a holding pattern. Waiting their turn to empty.

ROSE. (Empty.) Like an unfilled grave.

DAN *waters* ROSE. *Sound: beginning rainfall.*

AMY. Then a drip. Just one. A big, fat slug of a raindrop, slapping onto your hand. Then another, and another. Too fast to count. Too wet to shake off. All the dots joining up in a single sheet that hangs at your door for hours, for days, for weeks.

ROSE *is getting wet.*

The rain's supposed to wash things clean. But here, it washes them dirty. Everything drenched in dark. (*Pause.*) We live here.

DAN *stops sprinkling* ROSE.

DAN. We winna always.

AMY. No?

> ROSE *comes to realise the rain has stopped. Sound, quietly: sheep.*

ROSE. It doesn't rain for ever. It empties itself. It drains and dries. The roof's due in June. The plasterer's sent an estimate. There's stirring in the soil. Things afoot. Soft wee baa-lambs growing and wanting out to the air.

> DAN *hands* ROSE *the daffodils.*

> The tips are showing. The real tips of the wee wet flowers. It's the spring.

DAN. Cut.

ROSE. I'll put these back in the sideboard.

> ROSE *takes the camera and leaves.* DAN *moves the sofa back to its place.* AMY *helps.*

DAN. I could be him, for all you know. You've never met him. So how do you know I'm not? He could be writing all that stuff from anywhere. From next door.

> DAN *leaves.* AMY *returns to the computer.*

Scene Seven

in which Amy and Rafi almost put the knife in

AMY *is at the computer.*

AMY. Things – are – moving – in the heart of Paris. People are – bustling – in the heart of Paris. Bonjour, they say, at the station gate. Bonjour. Ça va. How are you? How are *you*? Is that a heart I see throbbing on your sleeve? I got it at the butcher's. I don't know what it's doing there. It isn't even attached. To anything. Not to me. Not to you. It's beating. A life of its own. I've tried to stop it.

> *Pause. A knock at the door: ddd. Pause.*

Hello?

RAFI. Hello?

AMY. Is that you?

RAFI. I think so. I may be wrong.

AMY. I'll be right there.

She checks herself in the mirror, pinches her cheeks, bites her lips, flattens her hair, opens the door. RAFI enters. He's wearing a T-shirt and combats.

Hi. Good to meet you.

RAFI. You too. Good place. Place is good. I just had a near-death experience. The birds. The birds. Throwing themselves under the wheels like suicides. Playing chicken like professionals.

AMY. You brought a car?

RAFI. A rental. Thought we could go someplace, see stuff, do stuff, eat stuff, say stuff, relaaax.

AMY. There isn't much to see round here.

RAFI. Here is good. In a quiet, empty kind of a way.

AMY. Everything got flattened. No castles. Not even ruins. Just ghosts.

RAFI. Ghosts are good. Whoo-hooo. Got somewhere I can crash?

AMY. Sure. The settee, if you like.

RAFI. OK. You OK with that?

AMY. I'm OK.

RAFI. You're OK. We're both OK. The rest of the planet sucks. Nice top.

AMY. Thanks.

RAFI. You lock your door.

AMY. Sometimes. It's wild country, out here. Bandit country.

RAFI. Wow. Banditos. Guerree-yas.

RAFI *helps himself to a banana from the fruit bowl.* AMY *does the same.*

Wow.

AMY. Wow.

RAFI. You look like your photograph.

AMY. I do?

RAFI. That's a first. They never look like the photograph.

AMY. You do, too. Sort of.

RAFI. I lost the mustache. Woke up one day and thought, what was I thinking? And then thought, whatever I was thinking, I was thinking *wrong*. Shaved off this side, took a look, left, right, left right, couldn't decide. Does it work? Does it *doesn't* work? But by then it was too late.

AMY. It's better. Without. Younger?

RAFI. Thanks.

AMY. You see a lot of photographs?

RAFI. Sure.

AMY. In Scotland?

RAFI. Let me see. Greenock, Lanark, Girvan, Arbuthnott, Tantallon, Unst, Troon, Coll, Mull, Erskine, Fidra . . .

AMY. Fidra?

RAFI. It's an island. Off North Berwick.

AMY. I thought it was just a rock.

RAFI. I guess she lied about her address. I waited a couple of hours. Checked out a couple of caves. Whoo-hooo! Anybody ho-ho-home? Man, that was a cold day.

AMY. You've had a few experiences.

RAFI. That's what it's about. Try 'em on for size, stretch, squeeze, flex your pecs. If she don't fit, pass her on.

AMY. How you talk. It's different to how you write.

RAFI. Talking is faster. Less time to think.

AMY. I'm more on the slow side, talkingwise.

RAFI. I noticed that. I'm draining flat just standing here.

AMY. It'll be a different pace from what you're used to.

RAFI. You know what? We are going to exhaust each other. We are going to drip each other dry. You with your slow-slow-slowcoach, me with my mo-mo-motormouth. Time takes no prisoners. I like to talk free. What turns you on?

AMY. Music.

RAFI. That's broad. Country? Western? Reggae? Rossini? Rock? Funk? Pop? Alcopop? Motown? Downtown? Blues dark? Blues light? A whiter shade of pale? Or do you make your own?

AMY. I'm not used to this.

RAFI. To what?

AMY. Meeting strangers. Talking to people I've never met.

RAFI. We met already. Just not flesh to flesh.

AMY. I suppose.

RAFI. Mind to mind, we met. Soul to soul. Mommaboard to poppaboard. We had a modern connection. Got any marihuana?

AMY. No.

RAFI. That's cool.

AMY. Is it?

RAFI *produces a knife and plays with it.*

RAFI. You know Portmahomack?

AMY. No.

RAFI. Is it far? Is it good?

AMY. I can't tell you. I've never been. Is that where you're heading?

RAFI. I guess so. In a while.

AMY. Would you like a cup of tea?

RAFI. Say that again.

AMY. Would you like a cup of tea?

RAFI. Again.

AMY. Would you like a cup of tea?

RAFI. It kills me. 'A cup of tea.' The accent. It's a different
    drink in that accent. A totally different drink. See: I say
    'tea', and you say . . .

AMY. Tea?

RAFI. Tea.

AMY. Tea?

RAFI. Tea. Hear that?

    They listen.

AMY. Tea.

    RAFI *begins sharpening the knife.*

RAFI. A totally different drink. It kills me. Say – there's this
    girl in Portmahomack. Leastways, she says she's a girl. I've
    lined her up for twelve. So, if you don't / mind

AMY. / It's OK.

RAFI. If you're really / OK

AMY. / I understand.

RAFI. If you're absolutely sure you won't be miffed, or pissed,
    or bitch about me behind my back . . .

AMY. Honestly. I don't mind. It's been great that you could
    come. It's been . . . different. And if you've got somewhere
    else to be, that's fine. Really. I won't take it the wrong way.

RAFI. Where would you like to lie?

AMY. Sorry?

RAFI. On the sofa? On the floor? Flopped across the table?

AMY. I don't follow.

RAFI. The shower's pretty popular. Or the master bedroom.
Have you got a master bed?

AMY. You're not planning / on . . . ?

RAFI. Planning? No. This is the next stage. The execution.

AMY. You're kidding.

RAFI. It's what I'm here for. Spent a lot of time, a lot of effort,
a lot of money on you. You better appreciate it.

AMY. I do. Up to a point.

RAFI. You naïve or something? You blind to the world out
there? You been watching the wrong kind of films? Black-
and-white and Sunday stuff? You been watching
anaesthetic? Didn't they tell you about people like me?

AMY. You sounded OK. You wrote OK.

RAFI. Oh Amy. My dear sweet white wine spritzer. How long
you been out of the world?

AMY. Two years.

RAFI. Two years. How long since you saw a city?

AMY. A year.

RAFI. How long since you went out?

AMY. Out?

RAFI. You got problems.

AMY. What do you mean – 'out'? A nightclub? The pub?

RAFI. Beyond the gate would be a start.

AMY. I don't go beyond the gate.

RAFI. Wanna talk about it?

AMY. Not really. It's a big gate. Hard to open. Gets stuck.
You can see a lot from that gate. There's a horse in the field.
It rolls on its back sometimes. Lies there and rolls on its

back and gets up again. They come to my gate. Everyone.
Postman, fish man, meat van, groceries once a week.
Electric people, gas people. Even God people. I get books,
food, clothes, air. I get seasonal veg and seasonal views
from the window. I get all the news I can take and more.
And visitors. I didn't think you'd come.

RAFI. You ordered me. Dispatch, postage, delivery to your
door. Here I am. Wanna bare your neck?

AMY. No. I'm not ready.

RAFI. I've a schedule to keep. Neck or ribs – it's your choice.

AMY. I didn't order this.

RAFI. I got a quota to catch. Just relax. I'll take care of things.

RAFI *grabs* AMY *and puts the knife to her throat.*

AMY. You can't –

RAFI. We can do this easy, we can do it hard.

AMY. You haven't given me a chance.

RAFI. You want returns? You want to try before you buy? You
want to start reading the small print in this life.

AMY. I haven't signed anything.

RAFI. Sure. It was somebody else wearing your body.

AMY. I want to see the paperwork.

RAFI. That's the trouble with this day and age. You can't even
be a contract killer without a contract. Jeez. It's in the car.

AMY. I have a right to see it.

RAFI. It won't make any difference. Don't make those big
eyes at me. She made those big eyes at me. I hate that.

RAFI *leaves.* AMY *slumps on the settee. The phone rings.*

AMY'S VOICE. Hello. You're through to Wordsworth. I'm
sorry we can't take your call right now – all our operators
are busy playing Solitaire. But leave your number and we'll
get back to you as soon as we've achieved cascade.

Scene Eight

in which Amy and Dan keep their traps shut

While LIEVRE *is speaking, there's a knock at the door.* DAN *enters.*

LIEVRE'S VOICE (*French accent*). This is Michel Lièvre. Mme McAllister? / Mme McAllister? (*Pause.*) If you are there, please can you reply immediately?

Pause. The answerphone beeps off.

DAN. / Do you want me to get that?

AMY. No.

DAN. I'll tell him you're out.

AMY. He knows I'm out.

DAN. Does he?

AMY. I'm not answering the phone.

DAN. What's the problem?

AMY. I'm not ready. I'll talk to him when I'm ready.

DAN. He won't go away. He's still *there*.

AMY. No he's not.

DAN. Shutting your eyes doesn't make things go away.

AMY. They do eventually.

AMY *turns her back.*

DAN. I'm still here. I'm still here and I'm talking to you.

AMY. Then shut up.

DAN. I can't seem to stop talking.

AMY. Shut up.

DAN. Bla bla bla bla bla bla . . . still talking. Still here.

AMY (*over*). La la la la la . . .

DAN *holds her.* AMY *tries to hit him.*

This is my space. This is my place. And if I can't choose who to have in it, where does that leave me? Where on earth can I be?

Pause. AMY *extricates herself.*

Not here. Not anywhere.

DAN. If I phoned first . . . left a message . . . would you pick it up?

AMY. Of course.

DAN. Would you?

AMY. I don't know.

DAN. Would you?

AMY. No!

DAN. Why not?

AMY. Because I need a break.

DAN. A break?

AMY. From you.

Pause.

DAN. You can have a break any time.

AMY. Can I?

DAN. Any time. Just go. Away. Out the door.

AMY. You know I –

DAN. Go on holiday.

AMY. Yeah. Like you.

DAN. This is not a holiday.

AMY. From yourself. From the rest of you. Because you'll go back. You'll go back and it'll still all be there. Your so-called mates and your so-called life and the scene.

DAN. 'Scene.'

AMY. Yes, I don't know shit about it. I don't know shit about you.

DAN. You don't want to.

AMY. Too right I don't. Because I like you. This you. The one you bring here. I'd fucking hate the rest.

DAN. So do I.

AMY. Sorry.

Pause.

I can't be the reason you stay off the . . . stay clean. Keeping your keys, your money. What kind of a game is that? You've got to do it yourself.

DAN. I can't.

AMY. You can. I know you can.

Pause.

I'm busy, Dan . . . I'm working. I can't fill your time for you.

DAN. I've too much of it. And you've too little. Hey – I could give you some of mine.

AMY. It'll pass.

DAN. It doesn't pass.

Pause.

I was in here last night.

AMY. I know.

DAN. I woke you.

AMY. I was awake.

DAN. Your clock's really loud. Like an axe on a woodblock. Slow. Deliberate. Keeping you waiting. Thump. Thump. It's bloody hard work, you know, keeping busy. It's the hardest thing. And I thought: I wonder what's the opposite of 'busy'? What's it called, this feeling? And your computer was on and

AMY. (I heard you.)

DAN. I did that thing, with the computer. You know what the opposite of 'busy' is?

AMY. Empty.

DAN. I knew. I just couldn't remember the word.

AMY. You could have come up. If you'd wanted to talk.

DAN. I didn't want to talk.

Pause.

AMY. I don't think they're opposites at all.

Pause.

DAN. This bloke. Why are you letting him come?

AMY. He asked.

DAN. You could have said no.

AMY. I could.

DAN *turns to leave.*

DAN. I can't go back. I need a life to go back to.

DAN *goes outside.* AMY *tidies ineffectually, finds her make-up bag, then sits.*

Scene Nine

in which Rose and Dan film the ghost of summer past

ROSE *enters wearing summer top, shorts and sunglasses on her head. She's carrying a beach bag and the camera. She rubs the front of her legs with instant fake tan.*

ROSE. I've had a gin. It'll help me to glow. Are you ready?

DAN. Go for it.

She gives DAN *the camera. From the beach bag she takes a sun hat and a parasol. She sits in position against the wall.*

DAN *lines up the shot.*

ROSE. No yet!

From the beachbag she retrieves a bottle of red nail varnish and starts painting her toenails. Gradually, the light changes to summer. Swallows and house martins in the distance.

I only do this in the summer. They look all naked without. Like wee streakers wi their hairy bits. I shave off the hairy bits. No point in making them all glamorous if they've still a moustache. Same wi the legs. Off wi the hobbit look – strrrppp! (*Mimes leg-waxing.*) On wi the plucked chicken. Much more attractive. And then a bit of basting wi oil, a bit of grilling on the beach and it's more: plucked *sun-dried* chicken. See, I'm a summer. Dark eyes, dark hair. I'm at my best bold and saturated. Fuschia and petrol. Scarlet and teal. Hot pink and African violet. If you put me in biscuit I'd look like a corpse wi the jaundies.

A jet rips overhead.

I remember you this high. Tripping on a baggie net twice your size. Near put my eye out. The minute you got out the car, you'd be tearing round the place like a dog let loose. Like you never got to play all year. I found a thing when I was papering. Must have been Mother did it. All your heights on the wall. And dates. From here to here.

DAN. I used to stand on tiptoe. She never noticed.

ROSE (*remembering*). Aye.

DAN. Summer.

ROSE. Better get on. Are you running?

DAN. Yeah. Action.

DAN *films.*

ROSE. I've a new roof now. The attic was thick wi bat crap. They've scraped the worst and covered the rest in loft insulation. They're replastered the stairwell and papered the hall and screeded the bathroom and wi your eyes screwed you could just about imagine it like a place you'd see on the telly. So I'm getting there. Getting there. The mood is lifting. I'm not as down as I was on my last contribution, all those months ago. So I'm having a wee drink to celebrate. Cheers!

DAN. Cut.

They exit.

Scene Ten

in which Amy and Rafi approach proximity

AMY *makes up her face.*

AMY. First, remove all unwanted debris, like so. Left to right, moving gradually in a circular motion. The wrist action should be smooth and firm. Take care not to miss any cracks. As you can see, the surface is now smooth and ready for screeding. Now apply the screed with firm, smooth movements, spreading all excess into any remaining crevices, to give a flat, primed surface. For those who prefer a matt finish, I like to advise the use of powder, like so. And so. And then, using a stencil brush, carefully stipple on a dash of colour. Not too much. Less is definitely more. Unless you're feeling reckless, or careless, or what-the-heck, in which case more is definitely more.

A knock at the door: dd.

God.

RAFI *enters, wearing jeans, T-shirt and spurs.*

RAFI. Howdy. I said howdy, purty lady. Seems to me purty lady's purty inhospitable. But that's just her way. I guess that's just her way.

AMY. Get lost.

AMY *changes her trackie bottoms into a skirt and sandals.*

RAFI. Purty lady's purty darn rude, too. Purty darn rude. Rude and inhospitable. That's some combination. Course, she don't appreciate that I'm mighty dusty from the long ride and one heck of a thirsty. She don't appreciate that I could just die for a pitcher of nice, cool water, maybe with a handful of cracked ice and a shake of bitters. But I reckon purty lady ain't got no nice, cool water. Purty lady ain't got no manners, neither. Come to think of it, she ain't even that purty. But that's just how it is round here. That's just how it is. Well, I'm heading north to Portmahomack. Been nice knowin you.

AMY. It's a rough day.

RAFI. Seems to me, you're feeling mighty sorry for yourself.

AMY. I'm OK.

RAFI. You sure don't look OK to me. Why, that smile of yours is stuck on all upside down.

AMY. Are you going to be relentlessly cheery here?

RAFI. I sure am.

AMY. I can't cope with that.

RAFI. Why, I don't know how to be any other way, ma'am. I had it beaten right outta me, soon I was born. The moment she saw the corners of my mouth turn southward, my dear departed granmama would holler 'Out in the yard, boy.' And then I'd go out into the yard and she'd be sharpening her special beating stick – the one with the rusty nails saved from the neighbour's picket fence. And she'd take me by the scruff of the shirt and lift her beating stick up high and beat that frown right out of me. Sometimes that frown would get the better of me, and turn into a holler or a howl or a tomcat wail. But then she'd beat me all the harder until I raised my head and smiled. The biggest smile you ever did see, ma'am. Now I suggest you take that frown and twist it around until it's pointing up the other way 'fore I get violent.

AMY. Where've you come from?

RAFI. Why, Oklahoma State, ma'am.

AMY. Tell me about Oklahoma State.

RAFI. Well, it's purty.

AMY. I guessed that much. Where were you born?

RAFI. In a purty little house with a white picket fence.

AMY. And roses round the door?

RAFI. Sure were.

AMY. And cactuses with their arms up dotted about the yard?

RAFI. That's right.

AMY. And those big dustballs blowing down the street?

RAFI. Getting all mixed up in the gunfights.

AMY. What's the name of the street?

RAFI. I don't rightly recall.

AMY. The district?

RAFI. It's clean gone out of my head.

AMY. The town?

RAFI. That I do know. I was born in the town of Surrey.

AMY. Surrey? The Surrey with the fringe on top?

RAFI. That's the one.

AMY. I hate to tell you this. That place doesn't exist. The whole of Oklahoma doesn't exist. You don't exist.

RAFI. If I were prone to confidence crises I guess I'd be floored right now.

AMY. Your hat doesn't exist.

RAFI. That's mighty hard to take in.

AMY. Your boots don't exist.

RAFI. Takes some swallowing.

AMY. Your hands, your feet, your legs, your arms, your head, your teeth don't exist.

RAFI. That don't seem to leave much left over. A ghost of me.
A shadow. A smile. Not much to show for a year of goin'
courtin'.

AMY. It's been that long?

RAFI. . . . once, twice, three times a day.

AMY. That much?

RAFI. Sometimes more, ma'am.

AMY. You're lying.

RAFI. Back and forth, words and words and words tumbling
like dust in a desert. Making a shape. Building a picture.
Pulling us this way, that way. Into focus. Getting to know
each other, inside and out again. And now I don't exist?

AMY. I'm sorry.

RAFI. Well, neither do you.

AMY. That's ridiculous.

RAFI. You've lied to me, Amy. Every word, you've lied. Lied
about your life, your work, your world, what you do, what
you like, what you think, what you dream.

AMY. What the hell do you know?

RAFI. You sold me a turkey. You sold yourself a turkey.
Because that high-flying, sweet-smelling, have-it-all-and-
then-some life of yours ain't happening.

AMY. You're wrong.

RAFI. Only in your head, ma'am. Only in your head.

    ROSE *enters. She's wearing a western frock. She speaks in
    her normal voice.*

ROSE. Can you spare a cup of sugar?

AMY. What are you doing here?

ROSE. It's for the best, dear.

RAFI. Pleased to meet you, ma'am.

ROSE. Hello there. See, she used to go out. She used to go out
and buy things. For the house. Paint and curtains and
cushions. And for herself. Clothes and shoes and eyeliner.

AMY. I had money.

ROSE. And she used to take care of herself. Do herself up nice
and keep her hair clean.

AMY. I had time.

ROSE. And now – well, I've tried. Trips here, wee suggestions.
Into the shops, off for a wander, away to the pub at night.

AMY. It's not my scene.

ROSE. She only has the one scene. It's the one outside the
window. That field. The hills, the horses. All framed.

RAFI. What happened, Amy?

AMY. Nothing.

ROSE. She never goes beyond the garden.

AMY. I'm no listening to this.

RAFI. What's beyond the garden?

AMY. Nothing is beyond the garden. Nothing important.
Nothing I need. Nothing I want. Nothing I can handle. OK?
Happy now? Cos I am. I sure am.

ROSE (*comforting* AMY). We can get you sorted, dear. Strip
you down, put in some new floorboards. A new roof and
downpipes. Sand you and stain you and varnish you all
shiny. Fill in the cracks and paper them over. Plumbing,
wiring, lighting, stencilling. New cream cushions with a
fringe on top.

DAN *enters and threatens with a gun.*

DAN. Leave her alone.

AMY. Jeez.

RAFI. Easy, sir.

ROSE. I'm only / trying to

DAN. / I said move.

AMY. It's my house.

DAN. You're coming with me.

RAFI. Don't do nothing hasty, now.

ROSE. Watch your step, laddie.

AMY. I'm no going anywhere.

DAN. He'll be here any minute.

AMY. Who?

DAN. The American.

RAFI. Oh lordy.

DAN. We've got to get out of here.

ROSE. I'm no having you shooting blood all over this carpet.

AMY. It's *my* carpet.

DAN. Shut it.

ROSE. Over my dead body.

> DAN *points the gun at* ROSE.

AMY. Dan!

RAFI. Easy now.

DAN. You've had it coming. Sticking your nose in. Looking in pockets. What do you know? What do you know about anything?

ROSE. Enough. It wouldn't look too good, would it? Wi your record?

DAN (*to* AMY). Come here.

AMY. You're kidding.

DAN. Give me the keys.

AMY. You're no getting them.

> DAN *grabs* AMY. *They struggle.*

DAN. You're trying to keep me here so that you've someone to be with. But I'm not staying. We're going out. We're leaving. Out the gate, down the road, away before he gets here.

ROSE. It's the world, you see. It's bigger than you wanted.

By now, they have closed in on AMY.

AMY. Get out of my head!

RAFI. Wait. Can you hear that?

ROSE. What is it?

Faint music begins: a waltz rhythm.

RAFI. Listen. Can you feel it?

DAN. Feel what?

RAFI. Yes! There it is!

AMY. There's nothing there!

ROSE (*re* RAFI). He's right. There's something . . .

DAN. Are you sure?

RAFI. It's growing.

ROSE. It is! Just a wee / feeling . . .

RAFI. / suspicion . . .

ROSE. Out on the edge there.

DAN. You sure?

ROSE. Positive.

RAFI. The familiar surge . . .

DAN. Hey! I'm getting it . . .

AMY. Getting what?

ROSE. The swelling . . .

RAFI. Climbing . . .

DAN. You're right.

ROSE. It's a force alright.

RAFI. Can't ignore it.

DAN. It's a big one . . .

RAFI. Sure is.

ROSE. It's a big one alright.

AMY. A big what?

RAFI/ROSE/DAN. A song!

AMY. Jeez-o.

ROSE. It's a / song.

RAFI. / Been building / up.

DAN. / Biding its / time.

ROSE. / Head of / steam.

RAFI. Waiting for its moment.

DAN. Has to come out.

ROSE. Can't keep it in.

> *A tune starts up – a waltz rhythm. Apart from* AMY, *they speak in time to the music.*

RAFI. It's one of those moments

DAN. It's one of those days

ROSE. When things get too much

RAFI.
  Just a little bit craz-y
  For ordinary words

ROSE.
  Everyday words
  Dreary old words
  Sneery old words

AMY. You're not going to –

ROSE. We are.

RAFI. We sure are.

DAN. Ain't no stopping us now.

AMY. Please. You are not going to –

ROSE (*sings in an unlikely, magnificent voice*). Sing!

DAN. Hey! It's here! She's started to (*Sings, ditto.*) Sing!

RAFI. Everyone's at it. Mind if I (*Sings, ditto.*) Sing!

   Their singing forms a chord.

ROSE/DAN/RAFI (*singing*). What shall we sing?

RAFI (*speaks*). Any old thing.

ROSE. Bout a girl?

DAN. And a boy!

RAFI. Bout a horse

ROSE. And a carriage

DAN. A doorbell

RAFI. A sleighbell

ROSE. A schnitzel

DAN. A marriage

RAFI. It really don't matter.

ROSE. It's nothing but patter.

ROSE/DAN/RAFI (*singing*). As long as we're singing a song.

   The music continues underneath. They speak over.

AMY. Please. Just stop. I can't stand it.

ROSE. We can't, dear.

DAN. It's unstoppable.

RAFI. If we don't let it out, it can do terrible damage.

ROSE. We'd turn purple.

DAN. Blow up like balloons.

RAFI. Explode into a thousand pieces.

ROSE. No very savoury.

AMY. You can explode all you damn well like. You're not real.

DAN. Want to risk it?

ROSE. We could try.

RAFI. It won't be purty.

The music swells. ROSE, DAN *and* RAFI *puff up, too, trying to hold in the song. It's causing them great pain. The music swells unbearably, inexorably to the next verse.*

The Song Song.

AMY. Whatever!

ROSE, DAN *and* RAFI *burst gratefully into a song chord (a 7th):*

RAFI. Song!

ROSE. Song!

DAN. Song!

Then:

DAN. Raindrops on roses

ROSE. And naughty nose-pickers

RAFI. Botox and detox

DAN. And car-bumper stickers

ROSE. Dogs in the night-time

RAFI. And answerphone pings

ROSE/DAN/RAFI. These are a few of our singable things.

ROSE. When it's one of those moments

DAN. One of those days

RAFI. When things get confus / ing

ROSE. / Just a little bit haz-y for

ROSE/DAN/RAFI. Words, words, odious words

DAN. We really don't care

RAFI. It's only hot air

ROSE/DAN/RAFI. As long as we're singing a song!

The music continues under:

RAFI (*re* AMY). She ain't singing.

DAN. Isn't even trying.

ROSE. Where's your gumption?

AMY. I can't sing.

ROSE/DAN/RAFI. Can't sing?

RAFI. Most everyone can sing.

DAN. Except lions

ROSE. And rabbits

DAN. And insects

RAFI. And even some of *those* can sing in the right surroundings.

AMY. Well, I can't.

ROSE. She's shy.

RAFI. That's sweet.

DAN. She needs encouragement.

ROSE/DAN/RAFI. You can do it! / It's easy! / Just go for it!

AMY. I can't sing.

ROSE. Have you ever tried?

DAN. Just let go.

RAFI. Believe in yourself.

AMY. Really?

RAFI. Sure.

ROSE. It's easy.

DAN. It works for me.

AMY. And you just . . . ?

RAFI. Go for it.

DAN. Let rip.

ROSE. Go with the flow.

DAN. Enter the zone.

ROSE. Everyone can sing.

RAFI. You just gotta feel it.

DAN. Everyone has a song.

RAFI. You just gotta find it.

DAN (*sings*). You just need some attitude.

ROSE. A sprinkle of latitude.

RAFI. A pinch of emphatitude.

AMY (*speaks*). Like, right now?

ROSE/DAN/RAFI. Now! / All *right*! / Go girl! / That's the spirit!

    AMY *tries to sing, almost believing she can do it. It's appalling.*

AMY (*sings*). Aaaaaaaah!

RAFI. That's . . . great.

DAN. It's a start.

ROSE. Try again.

AMY (*sings*). Aaaaaaaah.

ROSE. Harder.

AMY (*sings*). Aaaaaah!

DAN. Softer.

AMY. Aaaaaaah. (*Speaks.*) I can't.

RAFI. She's right.

DAN. She can't.

ROSE. Poor girl.

RAFI. How embarrassing.

DAN. How weird.

ROSE. How do you manage?

RAFI. What do you do with all those pent-up emotions?

DAN. Anger and fears / and

ROSE. / and hopes and frustrations / and

RAFI. / and anguish and heartache and being in love?

AMY. I have a cushion, OK? A cushion and a fist. Now leave me alone.

AMY *withdraws from the others.*

ROSE. That's sad.

DAN. Tragic.

RAFI. How does she cope?

ROSE. She doesn't.

AMY *screams.*

AMY. Aaaaaahhh!

ROSE. That's no way to behave.

RAFI. For a lady.

ROSE. We could all succumb to screaming.

DAN. Every day, we could succumb to screaming.

ROSE, DAN *and* RAFI *sing:*

ROSE. We could let it all out

RAFI. With a scream and a shout

ROSE. But somehow a song

DAN. That isn't too long is

   The answer

ROSE. The remedy

DAN. The tonic

RAFI. The salve

DAN. The booster

ROSE. The therapy

DAN. The bolster

RAFI. The valve

ROSE. Somehow a tune
   Sends us over the moon

ROSE/DAN/RAFI. It's what life is really about.

DAN. We don't get uptight

RAFI. If the lyrics ain't right

ROSE. We don't give a dime

DAN. If the lyrics don't rhyme.

ROSE (*speaking*). Hey! They just did!

RAFI. Whaddaya know?

DAN. It's a miracle!

ROSE (*singing*). We don't give a stuff

DAN. If the lyrics are duff

ROSE/DAN/RAFI. As long as we're singing a song!

RAFI (*speaks*). One more time!

   They sing:

DAN. Fill up your lungs

RAFI. Wriggle your tongues

ROSE. Moisten your gums

DAN. Position your thumbs (*In his braces.*)

RAFI. Loosen your hose

ROSE. And strike a good pose.

ROSE/DAN/RAFI (*speaking*). Like this? Or this? Or this? Or this?

ROSE (*singing*). We really don't worry

DAN. If the meaning's all blurry

RAFI. Jump into that surrey and
    Sing!

ROSE. Song!

DAN. Sing!

ROSE/DAN/RAFI.
    As long as we're swinging it
    As long as we're winging it
    As long as we're singing a song!

The song ends. Silence. The twitter of birds. A knock at the door.

AMY (*weary*). That's him.

RAFI. It's me. I've arrived.

AMY *goes to the door and opens it to a backlit silhouette.*

Blackout.

End of Act One.

ACT TWO

in which reality bites

A knock at the door. A second knock at the door. AMY *answers the door.*

AMY. Hello.

RAFI. Hi. I'm looking for –

AMY. Amy.

RAFI. Yes. Is she –

AMY. No. I mean –

RAFI. Around? Oh. But she'll be –

AMY. Back. Soon. She –

RAFI. Oh.

AMY. Said to tell you.

RAFI. Today?

AMY. Oh yes. Today. I think.

RAFI. Today? Because I'm only –

AMY. I know. She said.

RAFI. And you . . . ?

AMY. Yes.

RAFI. Are . . . ?

AMY. Hi.

RAFI. You look like her.

AMY. A bit.

RAFI. Very like her. According to the photo.

AMY. Oh.

RAFI. They don't always. Photos. Look like the people they represent. Or like other people they don't represent. As in your case.

AMY. No. It's –

RAFI. Confusing.

AMY. Sometimes.

RAFI. Amy's your . . . ?

AMY. Friend.

RAFI. Ah.

AMY. Sister, in fact.

RAFI. I see.

AMY. Which is why we –

RAFI. Look –

AMY. Yes.

RAFI. She's got a nice place here.

AMY. Yes. Thank you. I mean –

RAFI. Just as I imagined.

AMY. Is it?

RAFI. The horses from the window and the basket of logs and the loud swirly carpet and the coal burns.

AMY. You're not disappointed?

RAFI. On the contrary. I'm open. She's not gone to any trouble?

AMY. No trouble.

RAFI. For my visit.

AMY. Nothing special.

RAFI. Because it might be trouble.

AMY. Not at all.

RAFI. In the sense that it's an invasion. An invasion of one.

AMY. Man the barricades.

They laugh awkwardly.

You're Rafi.

RAFI. You know about me.

AMY. Not everything.

RAFI. You live here?

AMY. Yes. No. Sometimes.

RAFI. I don't mean to –

AMY. It's OK.

RAFI. Be –

AMY. Really.

RAFI. Intrusive.

AMY. No! Not at all.

RAFI. I confess I'm a bit –

AMY. Tired.

RAFI. Tired. And nervous. A bit nervous.

AMY. Oh?

RAFI. Yes.

AMY. Why?

RAFI. Because we've never –

AMY. met. I suppose.

RAFI. Not as such. Though in a sense –

AMY. In a way –

RAFI. We have.

Pause.

I guess she's probably nervous, too.

AMY. Probably.

Pause.

Would you like a cup of tea?

RAFI. I'm not sure.

AMY. Or coffee?

RAFI. I don't know.

AMY. Or something dilutable?

RAFI. It's not the drink per se that concerns me, frankly. It's the eggshells. Everywhere eggshells. I don't want to alarm you. I'm conscious of the strange . . . of the fragile nature of the encounter after all these weeks of correspondence, and I'm treading . . . tiptoeing around, verbally, wondering where this sudden formality has come from, and wondering – additionally – why you're pretending to be not Amy when it's patently obvious you are. And that makes me feel weird, and has possibly got us off to a rocky – to a challenging start. And I would like to suggest that we counter one pretence with another, ie that the first one, viz, you not being Amy, never happened, and we can start again as was.

AMY. I'm sorry.

RAFI. Not at all.

AMY. Really – you must think –

RAFI. I don't

AMY. I'm a bit –

RAFI. Absolutely not.

AMY. ever so slightly –

RAFI. No, nyet, niente.

AMY. You don't know what I'm going to say.

RAFI. Whatever it is, I'm not thinking it.

AMY. Oh. Thanks. Because a lot of people –

RAFI. I'm not a lot of people –

AMY. – would have wondered –

RAFI. – let them wonder –

AMY. why I'd do that.

RAFI. Call me exceptional.

AMY. Although you went along with it.

RAFI. Ah no.

AMY. Kept up the –

RAFI. Completely different.

AMY. pretence.

RAFI. A different thing entirely.

AMY. For ages. When you could have nipped it in the bud.

RAFI. I was trying to make you feel at ease, dammit.

AMY. I'm sorry. You did. You did, really. I felt really –

RAFI. I'm glad.

AMY. at ease.

RAFI. I did hope so.

Pause.

But to come back to your question, waiting, out there, unanswered, like an itch without a scratch – yes, I would.

AMY. Would what?

RAFI. The cup of tea. Like. Please.

AMY. How do you take it?

RAFI. I don't. I never do. It simply doesn't occur to me. But now I'm here – I'm thinking 'why the hell not'?

AMY. So . . . milk? Sugar?

RAFI. I have no idea.

AMY. Or lemon?

RAFI. Maybe lemon. Maybe that's how I'd take it, if I took it at all.

AMY. I don't have lemon.

RAFI. Or maybe not. I'm flexibility itself.

AMY. I take it with milk.

RAFI. Then I'll try it with milk.

AMY. Fine.

AMY. / Oh God. Oh God. 'I don't have lemon.' Why bring up lemon? You never have lemon.

RAFI. / Hell. Hell. Lemon, for Pete's sake. What's with the lemon? You never take lemon.

RAFI *produces a duty-free bottle.*

Or . . .

AMY. Oh.

RAFI. Too early?

AMY. Too soon.

RAFI. I'll pass. On the drink. Tea or otherwise.

AMY. I'll keep it for –

RAFI. (later)

Pause.

AMY. / Good flight?

RAFI. / Nice place.

AMY. / Thank you.

RAFI. / Yes.

RAFI/AMY. You first.

RAFI/AMY. No, you.

RAFI/AMY. I insist.

RAFI/AMY. Please.

They both make as if to speak and don't.

AMY. / Got you there.

RAFI. / Got you.

RAFI/AMY (*alarmed*). Stop it.

RAFI/AMY. *You* stop it.

AMY. / This is spooky.

RAFI. / This is scary.

AMY. / You said 'scary'.

RAFI. / You said 'spooky'.

RAFI/AMY. After you.

RAFI/AMY. OK.

RAFI/AMY. The chances of this happening are /

AMY. / ridiculously small

RAFI. / infinitesimal

AMY. / and shrinking by the minute.

RAFI. / and fading by the minute.

RAFI/AMY. Help.

Pause.

RAFI/AMY. Maybe it's a –

Pause.

RAFI/AMY. Maybe it's a –

Pause.

RAFI/AMY. You –

RAFI/AMY. No, you.

RAFI/AMY. a sign

Pause.

RAFI/AMY. a *good* sign

Pause.

RAFI/AMY. of some deep compatibility.

Pause.

RAFI/AMY. Oh.

They signal to each other: they each take a random book from the shelf, open a random page and, at a signal, begin randomly reading at the same time. They notice with delight that the synchronicity is broken.

AMY (*reads*). / 'My best fishing-memory is about some fish that I never caught. That's usual enough, I suppose.'

RAFI (*reads*). / 'She owned that, considering everything, she was not absolutely without inclination for the party.'

They gesture to establish that AMY *speaks first.*

AMY. The flight. Was it good?

RAFI. Yes, I suppose it was. It did the job and then some.

AMY. Oh.

RAFI. The stewards were unusually courteous and the chicken breast salad had some flavour and crunch. On the down side, I had no view. The ground was obscured by a thick layer of clouds.

AMY. What kind of clouds?

RAFI. Those solid ones. With a Latin name.

AMY. They all have a Latin name.

RAFI. Cumulo –

AMY. Cumulo –

RAFI. Cumulo, but not –

AMY. Nimbus. Something else.

RAFI. Grey and lumpy. Like a mattress below.

AMY. For birds to bounce on.

RAFI. And above –

AMY. The sky?

RAFI. But what a sky!

AMY. Blue?

RAFI. Bluer than that.

AMY. Because you were so close to it.

RAFI. Thick blue like a sandwich.

AMY. Close-range blue.

RAFI. Edible blue.

AMY. Touchable blue.

RAFI. Meaty blue.

AMY. You had a view. A view of blue.

RAFI. Yes.

AMY. And you landed . . . ?

RAFI. Through the clouds. We pierced them. We ploughed a path. We went down. And down. And down. To Edinburgh.

AMY. Safely.

RAFI. I don't land well at all. I don't land well at all. I forgot to. Remember that. Before we took off.

Pause.

We could go somewhere.

AMY. You're just here. Isn't here enough?

RAFI. It's small. (*Off her look.*) Great, but small.

AMY. You're used to bigger.

RAFI. It's not that.

AMY. Bigger, fancier, chic-er. I knew it.

RAFI. No!

AMY. 'More space.'

RAFI. There's plenty of space.

AMY. I have all the space I need.

RAFI. It's spacious.

AMY. More than I need.

RAFI. So roomy.

AMY. Too much, sometimes. Too much, for one.

RAFI. We'll stay here. For now.

Pause.

AMY. What have we done?

RAFI. Something / impulsive.

AMY. / I don't know what to / think.

RAFI. Something / risky.

AMY. / Is it even legal?

RAFI. Yes. I checked it out.

AMY. Oh.

Pause.

Where does this leave us?

RAFI. We need to talk.

AMY. Oh God. Yes. Let's talk.

RAFI. Everything is so –

AMY. I'll understand.

RAFI. So –

AMY. I won't be hurt.

RAFI. So unusual.

AMY. Not in the slightest –

RAFI. So –

AMY. We need to talk.

Silence.

RAFI. Where to begin?

AMY. Here. Now.

RAFI. I can't do small talk.

AMY. We're so beyond small talk.

RAFI. I fell in love, frankly.

AMY. Did you?

RAFI. I did.

AMY. So did I. Frankly.

Pause.

RAFI. With what, exactly?

AMY. With you.

RAFI. Oh.

AMY. Or a version of you.

RAFI. Oh. (*Pause.*) So did I.

AMY. Oh. With me? Or a version of me?

RAFI. Both.

AMY. Oh. (*Pause.*) Where does that leave us?

RAFI. Here.

AMY. Oh.

RAFI. In the same place.

AMY. Oh.

Pause.

Well. Hello. Really.

RAFI. Hello, really.

Pause.

I feel like shaking hands. Should we shake hands?

AMY. I don't know.

RAFI. Just a brief shake of hands.

AMY. It doesn't feel right.

RAFI. Bite the bullet?

AMY. You're putting me off.

RAFI. Too forward?

AMY. The bullets. And the biting. / It sounds –

RAFI. / A manner of speaking.

AMY. Aggressive.

RAFI. Forget I said it.

AMY. I can't.

RAFI. It's just a hand.

He offers a hand.

And yours.

AMY *reaches out, but withdraws her hand suddenly.*

AMY. It might have implications.

RAFI. What sort of implications?

AMY. Legal implications.

RAFI. What sort of legal implications?

AMY. I don't know. Sealing a deal.

RAFI. This is not a deal. This is hello.

AMY. This is not how I do hello. Not with people I care about.

RAFI. And you do care, about this, me, us?

AMY. I do. More than this. More than a handshake. A handshake is for business and bosses and passers-by. I'd have to say 'how are you' and 'pleased to meet you' and 'have a good trip?' and we've already seen that you've had a good trip with a view of clouds and mattresses and a safe piercing down to Edinburgh and is that all I am to you? A handshake?

RAFI. You want to hug?

AMY. Oh God.

RAFI. Not hug.

AMY. I don't know.

RAFI. We're not ready

AMY. For a hug

RAFI. Too close

AMY. Too much

RAFI. Too fast

AMY. Too soon

RAFI. Too fleshly.

AMY. What do you mean, 'too fleshly'?

RAFI. I mean –

AMY. Too fat?

RAFI. Did I say fat?

AMY. Too fat.

RAFI. Not fat.

AMY. Too much flesh.

RAFI. Not too much flesh.

AMY. Excessive flesh.

RAFI. By no means.

AMY. Abundant in the flesh department.

RAFI. Not at all.

AMY. More flesh than you expected.

RAFI. Just the right amount of flesh.

AMY. How do you know? How do you know how much flesh? We've never met.

Pause.

RAFI. You want a kiss.

AMY. I don't know. Maybe.

RAFI. On the cheek?

AMY. Possibly.

RAFI. On both cheeks?

AMY. I'm not sure.

RAFI. On the hand?

AMY. Not the hand.

RAFI. On the lips?

AMY. I'm thinking.

RAFI. Just gently.

AMY. Just gently.

RAFI. And my hands are . . . ?

AMY. By your side.

RAFI. Firmly by my side.

AMY. Except . . .

RAFI. Except . . . ?

AMY. When they . . .

RAFI. Move . . . ?

AMY. Away . . .

RAFI. From my side . . . ?

AMY. And up . . .

RAFI. Towards . . . ?

AMY. My . . .

RAFI. Your . . . ?

AMY/RAFI. Cheek.

Pause.

RAFI. Now?

AMY. Now . . .

A knock at the door. They freeze.

Oh.

RAFI. Ah.

AMY. I can't . . .

RAFI. While there's

AMY. Someone

RAFI. At the

Another knock.

AMY. Yes. Waiting.

RAFI. Insistent.

AMY. The moment is

RAFI. *was*

AMY. / gone.

RAFI. / disturbed.

They break away.

Were you expecting someone?

AMY. You. And now you're

RAFI. Here. So it can't be –

AMY. You.

RAFI. A fair assumption.

AMY. Unless

RAFI. Unless?

AMY. You're not you.

RAFI. No?

AMY. You're someone else.

RAFI. Who?

AMY. An intruder. Pretending to be / you

RAFI. / me. While the real / me

AMY. / you is outside, waiting.

An impatient knock at the door.

RAFI. It's not / me.

AMY. / you?

RAFI. I don't think so.

Pause.

Who is it?

AMY. I don't know. I won't know for certain until I open the door.

RAFI. It could be anyone.

AMY. In theory.

RAFI. Anyone at all. Out of the blue.

AMY. But in practice . . .

RAFI. I guess . . .

AMY. It could be the fishman or the postman or the postgirl or the meter man or the Securicor van bringing Amazon things or the religion men with suits and chins, in which case we could sit tight.

RAFI. Like now.

AMY. And they'll go away.

RAFI. Eventually.

They wait. The letter box creaks open.

AMY. But suspect it's not.

ROSE. Hellooooo.

AMY. I suspect it's next door.

RAFI. The voice is distinctive.

ROSE. Yooo hoooo.

AMY. The problem is, they know I'm here.

RAFI. Can they be sure?

AMY. They'll deduce . . .

RAFI. They'll deduce *me*?

AMY. They watched you come in.

RAFI. We could sit tight.

AMY. We could.

RAFI. Sit

AMY. tight.

They sit tight.

If we sit *too* tight, they'll worry.

ROSE (*worried*). Amy!

AMY. They'll think there's something wrong.

ROSE. Are you OK?

AMY. They'll panic.

ROSE. She's not answering.

AMY. They'll jump to conclusions.

ROSE. Something's happened.

AMY. Wrong conclusions.

ROSE. Something terrible's happened.

AMY. They'll be irrational.

ROSE. I can feel it in my water.

AMY. They'll become hysterical.

ROSE. She's dead. She's dead.

AMY. Accusations will fly.

ROSE. He's killed her. I knew it.

AMY. They'll get others involved.

ROSE. Do something! Get onto the police!

DAN. Out the way. Let me look.

AMY. So I have to –

RAFI. Open the door.

> AMY *opens the door.* ROSE *and* DAN *straighten up from letter-box height.* DAN *has the camcorder.*

ROSE. Hello, dear. We've come to borrow something.

DAN. Something autumny. Something / brown.

ROSE. / Sugar. Brown sugar.

AMY. There's a first.

ROSE. Everything's fine?

AMY. Everything's fine.

ROSE. Sure?

AMY. Sure.

ROSE. And why should it no be fine? A fine autumny day and the sun out fine and the leaves crisping fine and the fine cousin here to enjoy it with. (*To* RAFI.) Hello.

RAFI. Pleased to meet you.

ROSE. Me too. This is Dan.

> *They shake hands.*

We live here. Next door. And next next door.

RAFI. It's a fine place.

ROSE. It is. Though we don't notice, really. Don't appreciate. Not enough. (*Re* DAN.) He's filming. (*Tetchy.*) Honestly.

DAN. Just testing. The light.

ROSE. It takes someone else to really notice things. Point out the things you've stopped seeing. My bucket. I've got such a photogenic bucket. (*To* DAN.) Show him. The bucket. You wouldn't believe my bucket. It could star in its own film.

RAFI. Wow.

They look at the camera screen.

DAN. Back a bit.

ROSE. Before the compost bin.

DAN. It's the time of year. Makes everything look good.

ROSE. Autumn's a very forgiving time, lightwise.

RAFI. Golden hour.

DAN. Low light, long shadows.

RAFI. Wow.

ROSE. See?

RAFI. That's some . . . bucket?

ROSE. Isn't it just?

RAFI. It has its own halo.

DAN. I was pleased with that.

RAFI. The modelling . . . those vertical grooves . . . the way they're ribbed . . .

DAN. They stand out.

RAFI. They glow. They shimmer.

ROSE. Who'd have thought?

RAFI. And the handle. The way it arches out . . .

DAN. It's the angle.

ROSE. Let's see.

RAFI. Sculptural.

DAN. Not bad.

RAFI. And the way you pan round and catch the glint at the end there. Hand-held?

DAN. Hand-held.

RAFI. You have an eye. You certainly have an eye.

They shake hands.

Congratulations.

ROSE. Thank you.

They shake hands.

RAFI. You should see this, Amy.

AMY. It's a bucket.

RAFI. But what a bucket!

ROSE. To think it's been there all the time.

RAFI. It's out there?

DAN. Round the back.

RAFI. The garden?

DAN. Yeah.

RAFI. There's a garden?

DAN. I'll show you.

RAFI. Sure.

DAN. Now?

RAFI. Seize the moment.

Pause.

DAN (*re* AMY). Are you sure?

RAFI. Why not?

He takes his own video camera from his backpack.

It's new. I bought it for the trip. I haven't quite –

ROSE. It's easy. Point and shoot. They do all the thinking for you.

RAFI. Amy?

AMY. It's a bucket.

RAFI. I'll stay.

AMY. A bucket with a halo.

RAFI *hesitates.*

DAN. Come on.

RAFI. Thanks.

RAFI *and* DAN *exit.*

AMY. No contest.

ROSE. He's nice.

AMY. Don't go away.

ROSE. You're alright?

AMY. I don't know.

ROSE. He's come a long way.

AMY. Must be desperate.

ROSE. To see you.

AMY. No that you'd notice. Five minutes in the door and he's off to see a much more interesting, lively, film-star-looking, groovy, glowing, halo-wearing, tart-faced *bucket.*

ROSE. You're no making sense.

AMY. Am I not? Am I not am I not? Am I not?

ROSE. Sit down.

AMY. Why?

She sits.

ROSE. From the beginning.

AMY. We wrote. On the internet.

ROSE. Right.

AMY. We wrote a lot. A lotalot.

ROSE. Like penpals.

AMY. Every day, we wrote. Several times, we wrote.

ROSE. OK.

AMY. More and more.

ROSE. Back and forrit.

AMY. Like a conversation.

ROSE. Chatty, like.

AMY. Oh yes.

ROSE. And?

AMY. Then we got married. Remotely. Down the phone line.

ROSE. . . .

AMY. A fortnight ago. You were painting the roans.

ROSE *starts laughing.*

ROSE. Away.

AMY. It's funny.

ROSE. It's not funny.

AMY. It's not funny.

ROSE (*trying not to laugh*). I'm not . . .

AMY. No.

ROSE. I'm happy for you.

AMY. Thanks.

ROSE. Both of you. I'm just –

AMY. You don't believe me.

ROSE. Well, no. It's not legal.

AMY. It is.

ROSE. It / can't be.

AMY. / legal. In Mexico.

ROSE *stops laughing.*

ROSE. In Mexico? I'm too old for this.

AMY. Sorry, I –

ROSE. I'm too old for this world. All of a sudden.

AMY. Sit down.

ROSE. I was keeping up. With everything. Not understanding everything. But open to everything. Interested in everything. Digital this and buttons that and voices in India pretending to be in my kitchen.

AMY. It's OK.

ROSE. Don't we have to *be* anywhere any more?

Pause.

AMY. (He'll be hungry. It's a long flight.)

ROSE. No even a proper talk with the man.

AMY. (Then the long drive down.)

ROSE. No even getting a look at the man.

AMY. (Wrong side of the road.)

ROSE. Where's the romance in that?

AMY. In your head.

ROSE. In your head?

AMY. Where it always is.

ROSE. Oh no.

AMY. A wee bright picture.

ROSE. That's all?

AMY. He said things. Good things. I felt wanted. I felt happy. I felt sick. I felt what-the-heck.

ROSE. You felt lonely. Lonely's what you felt.

AMY. No.

ROSE. Lonely does funny things.

AMY. I love him.

ROSE. Aye well.

AMY. I do.

ROSE. You *think* you do.

AMY. What's the difference?

ROSE. What's the difference?

AMY. Aye. What is the bloody difference?

ROSE. Oh.

AMY. Maybe thinking's all it is.

ROSE. Ts.

AMY. Pictures.

ROSE. No.

AMY (*re her head*). Up here.

ROSE. That's a fillum. That's a fillum wi the heads cut out and your face gaping through the hole.

AMY. It feels like it's meant to feel.

ROSE. And where's the feel of the man in that? The chin and the cheek of him? The hands with the too-short nails and the morning-after breath of the night before and the fingers in your body and learning how it goes? How it goes . . . If it goes at all. That's love, if you've the stomach for't.

AMY. Says who?

ROSE. He's made a mistake. Coming here. Better to stay put. Better to stay perfect.

    DAN *and* RAFI *enter.*

DAN (*to* AMY). You're leaving.

AMY. Oh.

RAFI (*to* AMY). He didn't know.

DAN. Too right I didn't know.

RAFI. Did I do something wrong?

AMY. Doesn't matter.

DAN. You're leaving *here*?

AMY. That's the plan.

DAN. What plan?

AMY. I don't tell you everything.

DAN. But *him* you do. (*To* ROSE.) She's going to the States. With lover boy here.

ROSE. Well done.

DAN. Well done?

ROSE. Going out. It's high time.

DAN (*to* ROSE). She doesn't *go* out. (*To* RAFI.) She doesn't go out. Did you know *that*?

AMY. Yes.

RAFI (*to* AMY). We'll do it. Maybe not now. Maybe not today.

ROSE. You'll get there.

AMY. Aye.

ROSE (*to* DAN). Time we went. (*Pause.*) We're – making – a – fillum.

DAN. No.

ROSE. Plus (*To* AMY.) you need to talk to your husband.

DAN *laughs uncertainly.*

(*To* RAFI.) And you need to talk to the wife.

DAN. I've missed something.

ROSE. Come on.

DAN. What's going on?

AMY. I was going to tell you.

DAN. Tell me what?

AMY. He's not my cousin.

DAN. Blow me down.

AMY. He's my –

DAN. No way.

AMY. my husband.

RAFI. That's right.

Pause.

DAN. You're not joking.

AMY. No.

RAFI. I'm not the kind of guy who does wife jokes.

DAN. You're not any kind of anything. Not to her. You've only just met.

RAFI. I beg to differ.

DAN (*to* AMY). How long have you known him?

ROSE. It's been lovely to meet you.

RAFI. Long enough.

DAN (*to* AMY). How long?

AMY. A year.

DAN. You're nuts.

ROSE. It's really about time we were –

DAN. I want to hear this.

ROSE. It's none of our business.

RAFI (*to* AMY). Why not?

DAN. Aye. Why not?

AMY (*to* RAFI). OK.

RAFI. We met – oh, a year ago.

AMY. To the day.

RAFI. On the internet. We started writing. Just a little, at first. The odd exchange, just by chance, and then just by not-so-chance, then every day (didn't we?), once, twice, three times and more, until I decided – we decided – that we'd have to meet face to face. To dispel any doubts, you see. Not that we had any, deep down. But there are programmes – clever programmes – that simulate real human interaction, and you don't want to fall in love with one of those. And vice versa, of course. I had to find out whether the wonderful person that typed her way into my heart with so few spelling mistakes was real. And that's why I'm here.

DAN *shakes his head.*

In the following, < > signals quoted speech by other people.

RAFI. And then the wedding . . .

AMY. It was a big wedding.

RAFI. Hundreds of people turned up.

AMY. Thousands.

RAFI. From all over the world.

AMY. It was crowded.

RAFI. Chaotic.

AMY. Everybody brought flowers.

RAFI. Blue roses.

AMY. That was Angelface. And Ferengi brought –

RAFI. A thistle from the yard.

AMY. And a lily from Fatman's mother's grave.

RAFI. He said she wouldn't miss it.

AMY. And Slicer brought a crisan –

RAFI. Cristhm –

AMY. Crysthamum –

RAFI. Crithansumum –

AMY. He couldn't spell it.

RAFI. And the room was decked out in ruby silk –

AMY. – sixty chandeliers with beeswax candles –

RAFI. – Ragger burnt his eyebrows –

AMY. – getting them all lit up –

RAFI. – there was a whole lake of Moët –

AMY. – courtesy of Richbitch –

RAFI. – a lake of champagne –

AMY. – expensive champagne –

RAFI. – everyone diving in –

AMY. – <wheeee> –

RAFI. – <splosh> –

AMY. – <whooo> –

RAFI. – <splash> –

AMY. – mayhem –

RAFI. – chaos –

AMY. – and you wore the burgundy suit –

RAFI. – to match the décor. And you . . . oh you! Making an entrance (what an entrance) . . . white spangled dress, hair piled higher than a tower, neck all tucked with blossom. A vision.

AMY. You're sweet.

RAFI (*to* ROSE *and* DAN). You should have been there.

ROSE. We weren't invited.

RAFI. And then the bouquet.

AMY. It was big.

RAFI. Roses the size of plates.

AMY. The biggest ever.

RAFI. Greenery big as a bush.

AMY. I could hardly lift it.

RAFI. But you did.

AMY. I did. And they were all waiting.

RAFI. Jostling.

AMY. Elbowing each other.

RAFI. <you're blocking my view>

AMY. <this one's for me, sister>

RAFI. <outta the way, Fatman>

AMY. <you want to feel my claws?>

RAFI. And then she threw the bouquet.

AMY. On the count of three.

RAFI/AMY. One . . . two . . . three . . .

AMY. And up it went.

RAFI. twisting in the air

AMY. like it didn't know where to fall

RAFI. hanging for a moment

Pause.

AMY. And then it fell

RAFI. <careful below>

AMY. down and

RAFI. <here it comes>

AMY. down and

RAFI. <whoooo>

AMY. into all the

RAFI. all the

AMY. waiting hands.

RAFI. Hey! I caught it!

AMY. <that's not fair> they said.

RAFI. Would you believe it?

AMY. <that's cheating>

RAFI. You want to fight on my wedding day?

AMY. <no way> they said.

RAFI. <kiss the bride> they said.

AMY. Oh yes. They said.

RAFI. So I did.

AMY. You did.

> *For the first time,* AMY *and* RAFI *are comfortable looking at each other.*

DAN. You did *how*?

AMY. How?

RAFI. How?

AMY. 'How.'

RAFI. 'How.'

DAN. How?

AMY. It was just a kiss.

RAFI. 'Just a kiss.'

AMY. An ordinary kiss.

RAFI. Ordinary?

AMY. *In* that –

RAFI. It felt –

AMY. Real.

RAFI. Oh. Yes.

AMY. And

RAFI. We felt –

AMY. We?

RAFI. Connected.

AMY. Yes.

DAN. That's not an answer.

RAFI. Isn't it?

DAN. I want to *know*.

ROSE. Use your imagination.

   DAN *laughs.*

DAN. In their heads.

RAFI. Oh no.

AMY. He's taking the piss.

DAN. *I'm* taking the piss?

ROSE (*deciding to leave, to* RAFI). It's been nice meeting you.

   DAN *isn't budging.*

DAN. You're doing my head in.

RAFI (*to* ROSE). And you.

DAN. It's not legal, this stuff.

AMY. It is.

ROSE. In Mexico.

RAFI. Legal as a mortgage.

DAN. Hilarious.

RAFI. Maybe to you.

DAN. Who is he? Do you even know?

AMY. I do.

ROSE (*to* DAN). Are you coming?

DAN (*to* ROSE). Do you trust him?

ROSE. More than I trust you.

DAN. What's that mean?

ROSE. Come on.

AMY. I would have told you but –

DAN. But what?

AMY. You would have laughed.

DAN. No. I would have got you seen to.

AMY (*quiet*). Leave me alone.

RAFI. Amy.

DAN (*to* RAFI). What do you do when you're not invading people's lives?

ROSE. Now –

RAFI. I teach school.

DAN. Great. Just great.

AMY. This is my house.

DAN (*to* AMY, *re* RAFI). You believe that?

AMY. This is my house.

ROSE (*to* RAFI). It's the excitement.

DAN. He could say anything. Anything at all.

AMY. This is my room.

RAFI (*to* DAN). You're upsetting her.

DAN. *I'm* upsetting her?

RAFI. Take it easy.

AMY. This is my place.

ROSE. Shhh.

DAN (*to* AMY). Who is he?

AMY. I told you.

DAN. Some nutter.

RAFI. Hey.

DAN. What?

    RAFI *touches* DAN.

RAFI. Buddy –

DAN. No.

AMY. Stop it.

RAFI (*placatory*). Let's go outside.

DAN. Keep your hands off me.

    DAN *takes a swing at* RAFI. RAFI *punches him back.*

    Ah. You see, *that* . . .

AMY. Get out.

DAN. . . . *that* was interesting.

RAFI. Sorry.

DAN. Don't you reckon?

RAFI. I –

DAN. Your cousin has a temper.

AMY. You're a shit.

DAN. Hidden depths.

AMY. A shitface.

DAN. Bet you didn't know *that* about him. The human touch.

ROSE. I'll wallop you.

DAN (*re* AMY). *She* needs looking after.

AMY. Is that what you think?

DAN. I do.

AMY. That you look after *me*?

DAN. Every day.

AMY. No.

DAN. Every day, I look in. See how you are. Sitting there, glued to the screen –

AMY. Just waiting for your visits? No. I look after *you*. Talk to you. Keep you going. Fill your time. Keep your mind off the gear. I'm your displacement activity. If we weren't here looking after you, keeping your keys, hiding our money, you'd be off down the road like a shot.

DAN. We?

ROSE. Aye.

DAN (*to* AMY, *re* ROSE). How long has she known?

ROSE. Since I saw your prescription. Plus I saw your face when I was foiling up the chicken. (*To* RAFI.) He thought he was helping me to do up the house. No. Occupational therapy.

RAFI (*to* DAN). I didn't mean to hit you. Actually, it's the first time I've hit someone. In anger. Frightens me. That I could do that. No – I liked it. Or rather, I stand by it. That's what I mean. And if you want some verification –

RAFI *puts his hand into his breast pocket.* DAN *flinches.*

Woah – yes. Gun in here. I'm armed. It's part of our national costume, after all. Gonna shoot you dead.

As he speaks, RAFI *takes out a wallet and shows* DAN *an impressive bunch of plastic cards.*

Driver licence. Credit card. Travel card. Wine-store discount card. Library card. High school ID. Sport club ID, expired.

RAFI *pulls out a picture of his children and hands it to* ROSE.

My children.

AMY *(absent)*. Solly and Nicola.

(To ROSE.) They live with their mother.

He takes out a photo of AMY.

RAFI. And look who this is. How did this get here? *(To* AMY.) What do you know? She looks like you. Uncanny. *(To* ROSE.) Would you look at that? The spit and double.

RAFI *shows his organiser to* DAN.

There are names in here. Names, and addresses and telephone numbers. People out there. Friends, co-workers, tradesmen, whatever. People I've had a reason to put in this book. Pick one out. Go on. Give them a call. Ask them if they've heard of me. Ask them what I do for a living. Ask them what I look like. Ask about my ex-wife. Ask about my children. Ask about my convictions. Ask about my finances. Ask about my religion. Ask if I exist.

ROSE. Of course you do. Och.

ROSE *hugs* RAFI.

RAFI. I was starting to doubt.

ROSE. We should toast this. The Mexican wedding. Maybe later, when you've had a chance to – oh.

AMY. What?

ROSE. Nothing. I just wondered . . .

DAN. Go on. Ask them.

AMY. Ask what?

ROSE. I was just thinking.

AMY. Thinking what?

DAN. Thinking what *I* was thinking.

ROSE. Of course, you could always have it annulled.

RAFI. Ah.

AMY. Maybe.

RAFI. That depends.

AMY. It does.

RAFI. On whether . . .

AMY. Whether . . .

ROSE. Yes . . . ?

AMY. To have it annulled . . .

RAFI. There would have to be no . . .

AMY. That's the definition . . .

RAFI. – actual –

AMY. . . . of annulment . . .

RAFI. – specific –

AMY. . . . technically speaking . . .

ROSE. But you can't have . . . actually . . . without . . . you haven't had a chance to consecrate it.

RAFI. Consummate.

AMY. She wants to know –

RAFI. She means consummation.

AMY. I know what she means.

ROSE. (No that I'm fishing.)

AMY. whether we've –

RAFI. actually –

DAN. Have you shagged? She means have you shagged?

Pause.

Come on. Has your virtual relationship been virtually consummated?

Pause.

In fact, don't answer that. I don't want to know. (*Beat.*) I've put plenty girls in my head. Have them all the time. There's one – goes about, see her around . . . Not that she's special or different or does it for me in any big way. But she has no fucking clue what we've done up *here*. Done it all. You name it. Crazy things. Violent things. She smiles. Seems to like it. Not proud of that. Not proud of that at all. But let me get this clear – there is no connection between those two girls. No fucking connection. (*Beat.*) So I don't want to know.

DAN *leaves.*

ROSE. I do.

RAFI. Well . . .

AMY. Well . . .

ROSE. Well . . . ?

Pause.

RAFI. Yes, ma'am.

AMY. No . . .

RAFI. You didn't?

AMY. But did you . . . ?

RAFI. I thought . . .

AMY. Well, yes, but . . .

RAFI. You were . . .

AMY. . . . it wasn't . . .

RAFI. *there* . . .

AMY. . . . quite . . .

RAFI. . . . while I was . . .

AMY. *there* . . .

RAFI. *with* you . . .

AMY. at the same time as . . .

RAFI. . . . you were . . .

AMY. . . . with me . . .

RAFI. . . . at home . . .

AMY. . . . telling me . . .

RAFI. . . . thinking of . . .

AMY. . . . saying things . . .

RAFI. . . . touching me . . .

AMY. . . . in places . . .

RAFI. . . . where I / felt you . . .

AMY. / felt / things . . .

RAFI. / moving . . .

AMY. touching . . .

RAFI. climbing . . .

AMY. moving . . .

RAFI. touching . . .

AMY. Oh.

RAFI. Oh.

ROSE. Oh. You *have*.

   Pause.

   Congratulations.

RAFI. Thanks.

ROSE. I suppose it's none of my business.

AMY. No. It's private.

RAFI. You're right. Something / special

AMY. / personal.

RAFI. personal. But the way we met –

AMY. apart –

RAFI. in different places –

AMY. the *same* place –

RAFI. a shared / place –

AMY. / a private place –

RAFI. doesn't make it any less real.

AMY. Does it?

RAFI. Not to me.

> AMY *and* RAFI *almost manage to look at each other.*
> ROSE *gets up to leave. She's drawn into listening.*

> (*Absent.*) I love your mind.

AMY. You do?

RAFI. That it circles in that way. Wheels and turns and hooks into things and pulls them together, sometimes.

AMY. And you. Turning things over and looking at their underneaths, their insides, shaking them till they rattle, measuring them imperially, putting them into rows.

RAFI. Lifting things and passing them to me and saying 'look' and 'hey' and sometimes 'marvel'.

AMY. Cutting into things and finding their engines and numbering their parts.

RAFI. Making shapes I can't see.

AMY. Putting them into shape-shaped holes.

RAFI. Talking about things without names.

AMY. Giving them names I can't remember.

RAFI. Mixing your metaphors.

AMY. Laughing at metaphors.

RAFI. Making up metaphors.

AMY. Stealing my metaphors.

RAFI. And using them.

AMY. Uncredited.

RAFI. Sometimes.

AMY. Always.

RAFI. Twice.

AMY. You counted?

RAFI. Oh yes.

AMY. Oh yes.

RAFI. That you have a body at all is a wonderful bonus.

Pause. A wind gets up.

ROSE. They'll be here soon. The telly folk.

RAFI. Listen. The trees. They're dry.

ROSE. I'd best be going.

RAFI. You don't notice them drying. And then the wind gets up and they make a noise like summer's over.

ROSE. Like the start of term.

AMY. Don't go.

ROSE. You'll be fine. Away and kiss and be done with it.

AMY. It'll feel soft. And cold, maybe.

RAFI. We can start again.

AMY. Cold lips. A trace of wet. I'll want to wipe but I won't.

RAFI. Rewind. Do it better.

AMY. You'll smell of aftershave. A mask of aftershave. An expensive one with a name.

RAFI. I bought it on the plane.

AMY. I like it. Your chin will feel rough.

RAFI. I shaved in the morning. My other morning.

AMY. Rough and soft. This small wet place between us.

RAFI. Between our mouths.

AMY. Small wet mouths.

RAFI. Like molluscs and rocks.

AMY. Lips and limpets.

RAFI. I'm afraid it will be so / uneventful.

AMY. / nothing.

RAFI. So small.

Pause. Leaves tickle into the cottage. They listen.

ROSE. I remember the wee wet mouths thegither. Oh it was grand. Up in the bus shelter and hid ablow the golf brolly. His hand burrowing under my waistband and scratching up and up the way. I've no the breasts now but I've the feel of having them touched, by God. Like a lightning strike, it was. Like a tree struck sideways. And never since the same.

Pause.

I'll be away then.

AMY. I haven't got brown sugar.

ROSE. I don't need brown sugar.

RAFI. I don't take lemon in my tea.

ROSE leaves. A long pause. AMY and RAFI approach each other awkwardly. Once again, they can't meet each other's eyes. They break away from each other.

AMY. We can't do this.

RAFI. It's not easy.

AMY. From cold.

RAFI. Out of nowhere.

AMY. The blue like that.

RAFI. From a standing start.

AMY. I'm sorry.

RAFI. Me too.

The phone rings. The answerphone kicks in.

AMY'S VOICE. Hello. You're through to Wordsworth. I'm sorry – all our operators are busy trembling right now. System failure is imminent. Please leave your advice after the tone.

The answerphone beeps.

LIEVRE'S VOICE. This is Michel Lièvre. For God's sake. What's the hold-up now?

AMY. I'm scared to dive in. What should I do?

LIEVRE'S VOICE. How the hell should I know?

AMY. What would you do?

LIEVRE'S VOICE. Get on with it. And stop being such a wuss.

The answerphone stops.

AMY/RAFI. You know what?

AMY/RAFI. We shouldn't be standing.

AMY/RAFI. We should sit.

They smile.

AMY/RAFI. You first.

AMY/RAFI. No, you.

They gesture to break the synchronicity.

RAFI. Let's sit.

AMY. We were always sitting.

RAFI. Always.

AMY. At the screen.

RAFI. That's where we met.

AMY. Let's sit.

RAFI. Let's sit.

They sit separately but close.

AMY. It feels more

RAFI. more / right.

AMY. / more natural.

RAFI. It does.

AMY. My hands are itchy.

RAFI. Mine too.

AMY. Look. They're twitching on my knees.

RAFI. Trembling.

AMY. My fingers –

RAFI. – they're dancing.

AMY. Tap dancing. Patterns.

RAFI. Words.

AMY. I think so.

RAFI. What are they saying?

AMY. I can't tell.

RAFI. Shut your eyes.

AMY. Now?

RAFI. I won't look.

AMY. You'll stay there?

RAFI. Sure.

AMY. You won't move?

RAFI. Of course not. I'll write you back.

AMY. OK.

(With fingers typing on her knees.) Hello. 'Hello', it says.

RAFI *(ditto).* Hi – there. 'Hi there.'

AMY. How – are – you – doing – questionmark? It says
'questionmark'.

RAFI. I'm – good – exclamation mark.

AMY. Exclamation mark?

RAFI. Exclamation mark – exclamation mark. And – you – questionmark?

AMY. Surviving – smiley.

RAFI. You – smiled – exclamation mark.

AMY. Are – you – smiling – questionmark?

RAFI. I – sure – am – exclamation mark exclamation mark – smiley – exclamation mark.

AMY. Welcome – to – Scotland – exclamation mark.

RAFI. Wheeee – exclamation mark! I'm – here – exclamation mark.

AMY. I – missed – you – exclamation mark.

RAFI. You – too – smiley. You – too.

Their fingers move fast and fluently.

AMY. That – was – weird. Face – to – Face.

RAFI. We'll – get – used – to – it.

AMY. Are – you – OK – questionmark?

RAFI. Tired – comma – emotional – smiley.

AMY. <brackets – takes your hand – brackets> therethere.

RAFI. <brackets – squeezes your hand – brackets> thanks.

AMY. We – could – ask – the – weather – question – dotdotdot.

RAFI. It's – fair – over – here – and – U – questionmark?

AMY. Ha – ha – exclamation mark.

RAFI. <brackets> – hug.

AMY. <brackets> – fierce hug.

RAFI. <brackets> – I needed that.

AMY. <brackets> – Me too.

The 'typed' dialogue gradually speeds up to become more naturalistic.

RAFI. <takes her hand>

AMY. <takes his hand>

RAFI. <strokes her cheek>

AMY. <strokes his cheek>

RAFI. <moves in close>

AMY. <moves in closer>

RAFI. <bends over>

AMY. <bends up>

RAFI. <leans closer>

AMY. <and closer>

RAFI. <until>

AMY. <until>

RAFI. <my lips>

AMY. <your lips>

RAFI. <your lips>

AMY. <touch>

Pause.

RAFI. <I felt that>

AMY. <warm>

RAFI. <familiar>

AMY. <easy>

RAFI. <hello again>

AMY. <hello>

RAFI. <welcome back>

AMY. <you too>

RAFI (*types*). It's – nice – out.

AMY (*types*). Perfect – light.

RAFI. Golden – hour.

AMY. Flattering – shadows.

RAFI. <takes your hand>

AMY. <squeezes your hand>

RAFI. How – about – a – walk – questionmark?

AMY. Now – questionmark?

RAFI. Absolutely – exclamation mark.

AMY. OK – smiley.

RAFI. Where do you want to go – questionmark?

AMY. Out.

RAFI. <walks to the door> Come on then – exclamation mark.

AMY. I'm – coming.

RAFI. <flings the door open>

AMY. Wait – for me – exclamation mark.

RAFI. <stands on the threshold>

AMY. <walks to the threshold>

RAFI. <steps outside>

AMY. <steps>

RAFI. <holds out a hand>

AMY. <steps>

RAFI. <takes your hand>

AMY. <steps>

RAFI. <pulls>

AMY. <outside>

RAFI. <outside>

AMY. <outside>

Pause.

RAFI. You OK?

AMY. I'm fantabulous.

Lights dim on AMY *and* RAFI, *still on the sofa.*

End.

Scottish Anthologies from Nick Hern Books

A Nick Hern Book

Gorgeous Avatar first published in Great Britain as a paperback original in 2006 by Nick Hern Books Limited, 14 Larden Road, London W3 7ST in association with the Traverse Theatre, Edinburgh

Cover image: Euan Myles

Typeset by Country Setting, Kingsdown, Kent CT14 8ES
Printed and bound in Great Britain by Biddles, King's Lynn

A CIP catalogue record for this book is available from the British Library

ISBN-13   978 1 85459 936 0
ISBN-10   1 85459 936 4